Activity-Based Management

Activity-Based Management

Today's Powerful New Tool for Controlling Costs and Creating Profits

William H. Wiersema

amacom
American Management Association

New York • Atlanta • Boston • Chicago • Kansas City • San Francisco • Washington, D.C.
Brussels • Mexico City • Tokyo • Toronto

This publication is designed to provide accurate and authoritative
information in regard to the subject matter covered. It is sold with
the understanding that the publisher is not engaged in rendering legal, accounting, or other professional service. If legal advice or other
expert assistance is required, the services of a competent professional
person should be sought.

Library of Congress Cataloging-in-Publication Data

Wiersema, William H.
    Activity-based management / William H. Wiersema.
       p.   cm.
    Includes bibliogrpahical references and index.
    ISBN 0-8144-0251-8
    1. Activity-based costing.   2. Managerial accounting.
    I. Amacom.
  II. Title.
  HF5686.C8W4476   1995
  658.15'11—dc20   94-23628
                                        CIP

Printing number

10 9 8 7 6 5 4 3 2 1

To
Monica,
with love

Table of Contents

Part II ABM in Action: Practical Applications

List of Exhibits

Introduction
How This Book Will
Help You Fast-Track Costs
and Boost Profits

Because financial reports don't tell you when costs are out of line, continuing adherence to rigid standards can be costing your organization money. Critical on-line data from your actual operations is what you must have to be competitive in a business world of barracudas.

Giving you information that allows you to control costs is what activity-based management (ABM) is all about. ABM is a team-based information system that turns the control of costs over to *you*, not to accounting principles that leave out the details and interconnections. It allows you to track activities and the people involved in all your operations, whether yours is a manufacturing or a service business.

Here are some successful U.S. organizations that use the ABM system right now with dramatic results:

- AT&T
- Black & Decker
- Caterpillar Tractor
- General Electric
- General Motors
- Hewlett-Packard

And there are many others, large and small.

As a manager or owner, you want precise, constant product cost information, which is why you need this friendly manual and guide to controlling costs through activity-based management. This book shows you how to set up the system with minimal fuss and investment.

Best of all, you needn't scrap whatever system you use now. You will learn how to modify your present system to integrate the ABM competitive advantage. It also shows you how to motivate your accountants and financial people to set up team-oriented cost centers, all with the aim of promptly updating product or service costs.

Finally, this book will enhance your knowledge of what's going on, whether it's on the shop floor or in the service area, and show you how the system ferrets, sifts, and winnows information—in the final analysis, your most vital product!

Strict adherence to traditional budgeting or inflexible standards will kill your bottom line. Actual cost drivers or events are the key. Instead of burying costs like wounded ostriches, ABM laser beams what causes them—before the profit leaks start.

Seventeen Ways ABM Will Help You

1. Identify the true winners and losers in your product or service mix (see page 121).
2. Put predictability into your financial results (see page 3).
3. Identify seventeen missed opportunities for cost reduction (see Chapter 5).
4. Predict the impact of in- and outsourcing decisions (see page 139).
5. Know the five steps to immediate management of costs (see page 174).
6. Track real costs of product or service complexity (see page 166).
7. Understand how your organization consumes resources (see page 37).
8. Speed up what-if forecasting (see page 134).
9. Use key statistics to rally operations (see pages 13 and 169).
10. Compare costs of design alternatives (see page 164).
11. Improve accuracy in bidding, estimating, and pricing (see page 147).
12. Tailor reports to best suit your needs (see page 122).
13. Initiate the right incentive system (see page 160).
14. Create an environment of cost consciousness (see page 16).
15. Build in a focus on customers and niche markets with every activity (see page 10).
16. Control capacity without time reporting (see page 119).
17. Avoid the pitfalls of traditional systems (see page 179).

How This Book Is Organized

The book is organized into two parts, intended to facilitate your use and understanding of ABM systems. Part I introduces ABM and its uses in any industry environment. Part II takes you through core, in-depth case histories of ABM in action, using supporting tools and connections with the scheme of implementation cited in Part I. The focus throughout is on putting ABM to practical use in your company.

Acknowledgments

I owe a debt of gratitude to those who reviewed the manuscript. Their comments were invaluable in bringing the book to its final form. The reviewers included Peter Cieslak, Henry Wiersema, and those at AMACOM.

I would also like to thank the many others who provided support and encouragement. First and foremost, my wife, Monica. Also, Cecil Levy, Neal Fisher, Ross Pearlstein, Robert LeFevre, and the principals and staff of Miller, Cooper & Co., Ltd.

Part I

Activity-Based Management: What It Is and How It Works

1

Managing Costs Based on Fast, Real Information

As purveyors of useful information, traditional cost systems, with their one-size-fits-all approach, are totally inadequate for today's businesses: Not only are they unable to supply tools for controlling costs, they cannot provide managers with the information they need to run their businesses profitably. The only way to control costs is by identifying the relationships between expenditures and the activities that cause them, and that information is not and never was available from traditional cost systems.

As the most forward-looking companies around the world became more and more dissatisfied with the inability of traditional cost information systems to provide them with meaningful information, new ideas began to be developed to better provide data to support the emerging management programs (e.g., TQM) and especially to deal with the impact of overhead on true cost information. From these ideas came the concept of activity-based management (ABM).

Why Activity-Based Management?

More than just an accounting innovation, ABM provides information—information to help you design, cost, plan, market, and compete better than you've ever been able to do before. How can ABM promise so much? Because it provides an understanding of what *causes* costs.

Here are some of its many benefits:

- *It allows you to control costs.* ABM identifies *causes* of problems, and automatically alerts you to inefficiency. It doesn't rely on traditional time reporting or budgeting systems.
- *It furthers common objectives.* ABM fosters task-oriented team management. It eases communication by identifying relationships that are easily understood by all.

- *It furnishes decision support.* ABM provides you with the best available information for supporting all decisions involving costs, from buying new equipment to finding your competitive niche. Many practical applications in the form of case studies appear throughout the book.
- *It eliminates surprises.* With the information provided by an ABM system, month-end financial results can be predicted easily and accurately.
- *It enables you to create accurate product costs.* By directly linking up with financial results, ABM ensures a valid and up-to-date product costing system.

Activity Cost-Cause Approach

ABM uses **activity drivers,** the *quantitative* factors in your operation that best represent relationships between costs and activities. For example, *number* of purchase orders may serve as activity drivers for certain purchasing costs. As will be more fully explained in Chapter 2, activity drivers are used to assign support-activity costs to operating activities and to assign operating-activity costs to end products or services. They are the ideal focal points for controlling costs because:

- *They are objective.* Activity drivers are quantitative and measurable, so they prevent people from fooling themselves or each other regarding the attainment of goals.
- *They are meaningful.* Activity drivers have a cause-and-effect relationship with costs of activities. This relationship is what makes them stand out.
- *They are simple.* They are related to the underlying activities that everyone understands. This facilitates communication about goals and problems.
- *They are immediately apparent.* The number of driver units associated with a job can be easily determined by observing operations.

The use of activity drivers has immediate applications for improving budgeting, costing, niche assessment, cost management, and efficiency.

Understanding vs. Budgeting

Conventional budgeting can never achieve the level of control that ABM can. While conventional systems attempt to legislate cost behavior, ABM strives to understand it. Companies that carry budgeting to its logical extremes face harsh consequences. In one company, a standing joke was that only the accounting department ever made budget. During budget meetings, managers defensively contested the unfavorable variances attributed to them. Consequently, the discussion never got around to how to improve operations. Consistent with this atmosphere, employees seemed to show little creativity in their positions or loyalty to the company.

The following case study is based on a manufacturing operation, but it could just as well be from a service or other operation. (Service company examples are discussed more fully in Chapter 4.)

COIL FINISHING CO.: PRODUCTION DOWNTURN

The month-end reports are finally released and show a problem. Expenses are stable, but production is down. The top executives call a meeting, in which the line managers "responsible" for the apparent downturn are called in and chewed out. When the shouting stops, the line managers finally get across a point that the top brass seems to have missed. The *product mix* reflected in types of jobs run during the month varied significantly from that of the prior month. With some half-muffled apologies, the line managers are sent back to work. When they've left the room, the top executives privately express frustration about the budgeting system, which does not appear to provide meaningful information. The company turns to ABM as the only available alternative.

Results: The problem disappears. Budget discussions now focus on the operation itself, such as how to make improvements and avoid costs.

Does the problem presented here sound familiar? See the conventional approach to budgeting for Coil Finishing Co. in Exhibit 1-1. For the sake of simplicity, the only operations of concern are "cold rolling," "slitting setup," and "slitting run." (To generalize, rolling and slitting are unit-driven activities, as distinguished from setup, which is a batch-driven activity.) A comparison of the current and previous months shows that costs are stable but production as measured in pounds has dropped significantly. Under Coil's management-by-exception principle, the alarms go off, indicating need for investigation. How could productivity have dropped so radically?

As it turns out, it is the product mix, not the level of operations, that has actually changed. Exhibit 1-2 displays the activity-based management approach. Here, rolling activities relate to the number of passes through rollers, and slitting run to lineal footage. These relationships are perfectly clear when one is actually watching the operation. Rolling and slitting

Exhibit 1-1. Traditional Report: Coil Finishing Co.

Description	Current Month	Prior Month
Cold rolling:		
Costs incurred	$ 40,000	$ 40,000
Pounds produced	4,550,000	6,250,000
Cost per pound	$ .00879	$ .00640
Increase in cost per pound: 37%		
Slitting setup:		
Costs incurred	$ 16,000	$ 14,500
Pounds produced	4,550,000	6,250,000
Cost per pound	$ .00352	$ .00232
Increase in cost per pound: 52%		
Slitting run:		
Costs incurred	$ 22,000	$ 24,000
Pounds produced	4,550,000	6,250,000
Cost per pound	$ .00484	$ .00384
Increase in cost per pound: 26%		

A sample of the equivalent-units base in practice is the cost-per-pound analysis of a steel coil finishing company. As is seen in Exhibit 1-2, the base selected is inappropriate for gauging operating performance.

both use a coil of metal approximately a yard wide, similar to a roll of paper. Rolling reduces the thickness of the metal by passing it through rollers. Slitting divides the yard into narrower widths by cutting the coil of metal lengthwise.

In manufacturing, **setup** refers to the process of readying the machine for the next batch or lot; it includes such activities as adjusting the machine, loading material, and running test pieces from the new lot. The time span runs from the production of the last usable piece from the prior lot to the first usable piece of the current lot. The increase in *number* of setups is what has caused the seemingly lower pounds productivity shown in Exhibit 1-1. When you can see what happens when financial results are related to an incorrect base, the effects of the order and product mix become clear.

Traditional budgets based on equivalent unit costs like pounds are

Exhibit 1-2. ABM Report: Coil Finishing Co.

Description	Current Month	Prior Month
Cold rolling:		
Costs incurred	$ 40,000	$ 40,000
Number of passes	2,600	2,500
Cost per pass	$ 15.38	$ 16.00
Decrease in cost per pass: 4%		
Slitting setup:		
Costs incurred	$ 16,000	$ 14,500
Number of setups	510	475
Cost per setup	$ 31.37	$ 30.53
Increase in cost per setup: 3%		
Slitting run:		
Costs incurred	$ 22,000	$ 24,000
Footage produced	1,330,000	1,370,000
Cost per foot	$ .0165	$ .0175
Decrease in cost per foot: 6%		

Simply changing the bases from pounds to the more appropriate passes, setups, and footage makes a drastic difference in assessing performance. Here, results between months appear stable, showing that the *mix of products run* fully accounts for the problems indicated by per pound costing.

highly fluctuating and unpredictable because of the incongruity between the activity and the base used to apply costs. Once activity drivers are brought in and customized to suit the operation, the product mix begins to show a wide range of profitability. Any decision based on the prior method of determining costs must be reexamined.

ABM is appropriate for practically any operation. But traditional accounting tends to average all costs as if they were unit-driven. Batch-driven activities, however, occur in almost any industry. All service projects, for example, include similar activities regardless of size. Examples of batch-driven costs in an administrative setting are order processing and billing. Regardless of the size or makeup of the order, certain functions occur.

At Coil Finishing Co., activities and activity drivers are as follows:

Activity ("Cost")	Activity Driver ("Cause")
Cold rolling	Number of passes
Slitting setup	Number of setups
Slitting run	Lineal footage produced

After rounding, the following costs per unit of activity driver are:

Activity Driver	Cost per Driver
Rolling pass	16.00
Slitting setup	31.00
Slitting footage	.017

What can you do with this information? The next sections are only the beginning!

Implications for Costing

Traditional cost systems lead to distortion of information, causing organizations to drop profitable products and expand unprofitable ones. Perhaps your system undercosts custom, low-volume, or small orders, causing overstated profitability. Or you may be unknowingly giving away special customer services. Many examples of such problems and how to correct them are presented in upcoming chapters.

More and more companies are experiencing rising costs, which are eating away at profits, but they have no way of analyzing why. According to their cost information, products are as profitable as ever.

ANYCO, USA: DIMINISHED COMPETITIVENESS

Every year, Anyco's position in its industry diminishes further. The product mix has shifted toward low-volume and custom work, because the company's cost system makes them appear more profitable. Consistent undercosting has led to underpricing. Now, management would like to emphasize Anyco's most profitable products and operations, but without adequate detailed cost information, it has nowhere to start. Frustrated, management decides it's time for ABM.

Results: For the first time, there is relevant information that can be used to support management's decisions. With better information, management can now consider issues in detail. Anyco is well on its way to recovery.

Where do the detailed costs for ABM come from? Answer: From the same place as the information used in controlling them. The following is an example of how the same cost-per-unit-of-activity-driver information used in the budgeting examples can be used in detailed costing. Say an order has the following activity-driver characteristics:

- Two cold rolling passes
- One slitting setup
- 2,500 lineal feet slit

Using the costs per activity driver identified previously, you can determine the cost of the order as follows:

Cold rolling (2 @ 16.00)	$ 32
Slitting setup (1 @ 31.00)	31
Slitting run (2,500 @ .017)	43
Total order cost	$106

Two different 10,000-pound orders are compared in Exhibit 1-3. Product mix has a significant effect. The weight of the order again proves to be irrelevant in costing. When weight is held constant, the true activity drivers can show how significantly costs vary. The analysis has immediate implications for profitability and pricing decisions.

This approach is quite revolutionary when compared to the traditional costing shown in Exhibit 1-4, which uses pounds as the equivalent unit of production. If weight is used, orders for the same number of pounds bear equal costs regardless of setup, footage, or number of passes. As demonstrated in Exhibit 1-3, weight clearly does not drive costs. Companies using a system where it *is* used to drive costs may develop different markups for different products in an attempt to gain some semblance of

Exhibit 1-3. Sample Estimating Form, ABM Approach: Coil Finishing Co.

Description	Rate	Usage	Order A Extension	Order B Extension
Cold rolling	$16/pass	6	$ 96	
		4		$ 64
Slitting setup	$31/setup	2	62	
		1		31
Slitting run	$.017/foot	2,900	49	
		2,100		36
Cost of processing 10,000 lbs.			$207	$131

When calculated under ABM, the effect of product mix proves significant. Production tracked in pounds (see Exhibit 1-4) does not correlate with financial results, or with cost estimating.

reality. But what they fail to determine is the actual costs on which to base the markups.

Product costs should always reflect setup. Short production runs must fully bear the costs they cause; setup of $31 spread over 10,000 feet of slitting is much less costly than $31 spread over 100. You can then reflect setup and batch-related costs in minimum-order limits or allow volume discounts to discourage small-order business that may be unprofitable.

Also significant to the exhibit is the fact that selling prices of certain metal products may not vary exactly with gauge or width. Yet, as the cost model illustrates, it takes much more operating effort, and thus costs more, to produce thin-gauge material. If managers cannot price accordingly, they should at least recognize the work as less profitable and accordingly deemphasize it in marketing efforts.

Finding Your Niche

A niche market is one in which a company's capabilities exceed those of competitors in meeting the needs of a group of customers. Niches may

Exhibit 1-4. Sample Estimating Form, Traditional Approach: Coil Finishing Co.

Description	Rate	Usage	Order A Extension	Order B Extension
Cold rolling	$.007/lb.	10,000	$ 70	
		10,000		$ 70
Slitting setup	$.004/lb.	10,000	40	
		10,000		40
Slitting run	$.004/lb.	10,000	40	
		10,000		40
Total			$150	$150

Expanding on the earlier example, costing techniques that prove inadequate and non-predictive for budgeting will also be inadequate for cost estimating. Here, pounds is used as an equivalent unit, although that base does not reflect the operations.

originate in competitive advantages in serving certain markets. Competitive advantages may take the form of the following:

- ◆ Price
- ◆ Reputation
- ◆ Advanced technology
- ◆ Superior quality
- ◆ Service, such as delivery or support after sale
- ◆ Flexibility or customization

As times change, so do niche markets. Department stores began to have problems when they failed to recognize that the age of mass merchandising was over. Today, there is a trend toward customization. The black Model T's that satisfied a previous generation would not make it today. Companies that deceive themselves into thinking that they can continue to compete on mass production, and ignore the demands of today's customers, are doomed. Your goal should be to find the niche market best suited to your capabilities.

The absence of good cost information, however, is likely to pinpoint false niches. Custom work or small orders may appear to be highly profitable because traditional systems undercost them. The potential effects for a small-order, thin-gauge customer are illustrated in Exhibit 1-5. Customer B is unprofitable because of the large number of passes required on a per-foot basis to obtain the desired gauge reduction and the extra setups needed to accommodate numerous small orders. In contrast, customer A consumes fewer of these resources, resulting in higher profitability for the company.

Even companies that do not pursue lowest price should nonetheless minimize costs of any direction chosen. For example, offering special terms on accounts receivable or warehousing extra inventory for timely delivery may be a competitive advantage for distributors. The question

Exhibit 1-5. Customer Profitability: Coil Finishing Co.

| | ACTIVITY-DRIVER QUANTITIES (data in thousands) | | |
Activity/Driver	Customer A	Customer B	Others
Cold rolling/pass	6.0	9.0	25.0
Slitting setup/setup	1.0	5.0	10.0
Slitting run/feet	7,500	7,500	30,000

| | | EXTENDED COSTS (data in thousands) | | |
Activity	Rate	Customer A	Customer B	Others
Cold rolling	$16.00	$96	$144	$400
Slitting setup	31.00	31	155	310
Slitting run	.017	128	128	510
Customer service	direct	20	40	100
Total		$275	$467	$1,320
Cost per foot		.0367	.0623	.0440
Selling price per foot		.0530	.0530	.0530
Profit (loss) per foot		.0163	(.0093)	.0090

Customer analysis reveals losses incurred in servicing customer B. They arise from small orders of thin-gauge material, which cause frequent setups and additional cold-rolling passes. Customer B's customer service consumption is also higher than customer A's.

not answered in traditional systems is where to stop, i.e., what is the optimum profit level? ABM makes the trade-off visible. The costs of carrying the additional assets can be balanced against the benefits obtained. With trade-offs explicitly quantified, managers can take an informed risk. As long as higher profits on sales cover the costs, the strategy is worth pursuing.

The key to discovering your niche markets and competitive advantage is to thoroughly understand product and customer profitability. Traditional systems are likely to take companies off course. Redressing this problem calls for an objective reevaluation of the costing and information systems currently in place, to discover where distortions occur and how they might be corrected. When managers switch to ABM, cost-estimating systems become linked to financial reporting through budgeting. See how the information in Exhibit 1-2 was used in Exhibit 1-3: Costs at a detail level came directly from a budget that was proved predictive by being so close to actual results for the two months illustrated. New niches begin to emerge as others fall by the wayside.

Key Statistics

Simply identifying inefficiency is not enough. You need to understand and communicate its causes. As the president of a steel manufacturer once told me, "Tell me what's causing the problem, then let us solve it." When causes and trade-offs become explicit, the solutions and improvements follow easily.

For ongoing improvement, you must make the causes visible to the organization as focal points for improvement. This is where **key statistics** come in.

Key statistics help you to attain business goals, from improved efficiency to customer service. These are numbers elevated to a level of communication as critical to attaining organizational goals. A key statistic could be cost per setup, one or more activity drivers, cost per unit of activity driver, or end product or service costs. ABM identifies these key indicators. ABM is ideally suited to support key statistics because it provides valid, ongoing results.

In managing costs, you can select several activity drivers at a time as a focus for reducing costs. Everyone should be aware of targets and actual performance. For some operations, setup statistics may function as key indicators of efficiency. For others, it may be overtime. Still others might want to focus on time elapsed from providing services until collection from customers (see the compilation of information on this very broad topic in Compendium I). Under activity-based management, controllable costs, once buried in financial report categories of direct labor and overhead, are brought into view for the first time.

Of course activity drivers should be adapted to changing operational needs. See how Coil Finishing Co., having dealt with the setup issue, now moves on to the generation of scrap.

COIL FINISHING CO.: OFF-FALL INVENTORY

In its slitting operation, Coil Finishing Co. generates off-fall (leftover) material in filling customer orders. The off-fall inventory builds up, but no one will admit responsibility. "It's the product mix that prevents us from using the material more efficiently," the schedulers say.

The company decides to implement ABM.

Results: By pointing out the real cause of the problem, ABM enables the company to support a continuous improvement program to eliminate the problem. By changing scheduling and order policies, off-fall is reduced to nearly zero, without a corresponding decrease in sales volume.

As the cash tied up in off-fall increases, managers may desire increased control. Although inventory aging helps, daily production reporting can formulate short-term targets for control. The percentage of off-fall to production could be derived from yield reports or comparison of raw material charges to goods completed. The key statistics could be accumulated as illustrated in Exhibit 1-6. Departures from targets must be approved with causes documented.

Once you place responsibility and target operations, you can identify the orders or customers that cause the costs and charge them accordingly. If customers who cause inefficiency like rework and scrap by requiring complex products will not accept your attempts to recover the loss, your next step is to consider discontinuing the work.

Waste: Unnecessary or Mismatched Demands

Inefficiency can be targeted in the same way. It means rethinking and analyzing the process. What's really essential in meeting your goal of satisfying the customer? What isn't? For example, if moving material from here to there doesn't add value, why not trim that distance by reconfiguring the layout?

Exhibit 1-6. Off-Fall Tracking for a Manufacturer

	Material Consumed	Off-Fall Generated	Percent
Day 13	200,000	18,000	9%
Previous day	250,000	30,000	12
Target			8

Generation of off-fall material is a continuing operating issue for steel services. Given statistics such as those exhibited here, where can you place the blame? sales? manufacturing? purchasing? other areas? Probably all are responsible to some degree. A team effort will be necessary to eradicate the problem.

Once ABM is implemented, you no longer have to ferret out the causes of inefficiency. Activities that do not contribute to the end product may just as well not exist.

Managing costs means reducing workload to what's actually necessary and adjusting capacity to necessary workload. Why waste a resource when its usage might have been avoided through better process, design, or other decisions? Why include work that is unnecessary? Why add costs to fill an immediate need for extra capacity, such as costs to expedite a vendor delivery by Federal Express, or costs that continue when work is not there?

Understanding costs amounts to being able to measure demands made on resources. In Exhibits 1-1 and 1-2, the demands that the particular product mix places on the company's resources are almost identical, although the output and its sales value may vary significantly.

We can conclude that reducing setups frees up resources, which now become available for running more material and increasing throughput. The result is a decrease in workload without a decrease in productive output.

Let's cover the two ways of analyzing and eliminating inefficiency in more detail.

1. *Reducing workload.* Look at inefficiency as an unnecessary demand on resources. Consider slitting setups. Each setup causes a certain cost that is now visible. Once you're aware of this cost, you can consider reduc-

ing the number of setups or the amount of cost incurred for each one. How much potential for savings would come from a training program designed to reduce setup effort by 25 percent? How much from dedicating tools or fixtures to certain designs? ABM gives you the answers!

2. *Adjusting capacity.* The other type of inefficiency occurs when workload does not match capacity to do work, taking the form of additional costs. If resources are short in relation to workload, you may have to expedite vendor deliveries, incur overtime, or farm out operations. If resources are excessive, you may have to deal with idle capacity in labor and equipment and the additional costs of carrying excess inventories of raw materials.

Visualize a scale on which you place a load of work. If capacity balances workload, your cost per output is minimal. If the scale tips one way or the other, costs increase.

There is nothing wrong with excesses per se; a strategy of customer service may bring in sufficient profitable business to outweigh the costs of extra capacity in terms of people, inventory, or machines. The key is to keep costs to a minimum and still meet service objectives.

A New Attitude toward Costs

The ideal environment for implementing ABM includes:

- Goals visible to all levels in the organization in the form of budgets and targets.
- Team efforts in achieving budgets, backed by incentives and latitude in the means. These have proved to be effective in diverse environments, and stand in contrast to the isolation of individual incentives.
- An attitude of questioning, and of welcoming suggestions. Employees must know that their suggestions will make a difference.

As with any other major change, expect resistance. The best way to overcome resistance is to depersonalize it. The culprit is not the estimator, cost accountant, or plant manager; it is the lack of methodology.

The same applies to the inefficiencies that the new system may uncover. Inefficiency, not any individual or group, is the enemy. Don't pinpoint blame; prevent recurrence. Now that information is available to expose inefficiency, it's time to do your best to eradicate it, boost the company's bottom line, and share in an incentive for your team's contribution!

ABM implementation must be cross-functional, meaning it should involve all affected. This creates a cost-consciousness throughout. Those using and benefiting from the system must take "ownership" of their jobs. Any system that is intended to improve operations must involve operations people in its design and implementation. Otherwise, the system will be as foreign to operations as are the old ways of costing. Unlike traditional budgeting, variances under ABM lead to searches for undisclosed bases for applying costs. Pinpointing an additional driver could explain the difference. Once the fallacies of the traditional systems are exposed and the new goals clarified, the task of implementing the new system begins.

Creation of Timely Information

As you'll see, the ABM model is self-validating, so accurate and timely data will be available for continual decision making. Budgets can even be related to daily production for detailed assessment of operational performance. For a particular project or department, you can at any time compare actual drivers-to-date either to budgeted drivers or to activity costs. Traditional systems provide this information only about direct labor.

With predictable financial information, you will know costs consumed based on observed activity-driver quantities. No more month-end surprises!

Looking Ahead

The implications of activity-based management for product design, outsourcing decisions, entering joint ventures, and identifying niches will become clear in later chapters. Uses of the new information are limited only by your creativity.

What emerges from this process is an enhanced understanding of your cost structure. The behaviors identified are unique to your organization. Within these data lies the key to your competitive advantages in the marketplace.

That is the idea of activity-based management. The objective is not only to provide product costing but to improve management reporting, production efficiency, and cost control by relating costs to their causes. In short, it affects the most important functions in your organization.

2

Integrating ABM
into Your Organization

Before we build a basic ABM model, we'll start off with a few key terms, to be refined in Chapter 3.

Key Terms

Activities

Activities are simply the significant tasks that consume resources. For example, from the following table, we see that at Coil Finishing Co., cold rolling, slitting setup, and slitting run are major operating activities that consume resources.

Activity ("Cost")	Driver ("Cause")	Cost per Driver
Cold rolling	Rolling passes	16.00
Slitting setup	Slitting setups	31.00
Slitting run	Slitting footage	.017

These are so-called **direct activities** that go directly into end products or services.

The rates (or costs per unit of activity driver) derived for the activities include intermediate activities, known as **support activities.** Exhibit 2-1 breaks down these activities for Coil Finishing Co. The support activities category commonly includes activities pertaining to management, occupancy, and maintenance that must be assigned to direct activities to obtain end-item costs.

Exhibit 2-1. Activity-Driver Costs: Coil Finishing Co.

Activity	Total	Cold Rolling	Slitting Run	Slitting Setup
Direct:				
Labor	$ 250,000	$112,500	$ 75,000	$ 62,500
Supplies	130,000	96,000	8,400	25,600
Support:				
Supervisory	140,000	31,500	21,000	87,500
Rent	120,000	40,000	43,200	36,800
Utilities	90,000	50,000	35,400	4,600
Maintenance	120,000	70,000	40,000	10,000
Depreciation	150,000	100,000	27,000	23,000
Total	$1,000,000	$500,000	$250,000	$250,000
Activity driver		passes	footage	setups
Driver quantity		31,250	15,000,000	8,065
Costing rate		16.00	0.017	31.00

This exhibit shows the calculation of the costing rates used in Chapter 1 for the sample company.

Assignment of support activity costs to direct ones is known as **level I assignment;** assignment of direct activities to drivers for end-item costing is known as **level II assignment.** Exhibit 2-2 gives percentages of cost by activity. It would be well worth your while to study this exhibit very carefully, as it summarizes many ideas that will be illustrated in detail in the rest of the chapter. The basic idea is that all supporting and direct activity costs have been assigned, in this case to the three direct activities of cold rolling, slitting setup, and slitting run. The costs of the activities then are related to the appropriate activity drivers of passes, footage, and setups, respectively, to derive a cost per unit of activity driver. This is the essential amount found in all ABM applications, from detailed costing to budgeting. Note the large variations, particularly in direct labor. A common fallacy perpetuated by traditional costing systems is that total costs follow labor. This is certainly not the case for Coil Finishing Co., or any other multioperation or multiproduct company for that matter.

Exhibit 2-2. Activity Composition: Coil Finishing Co.

Activity	Cold Rolling	Slitting Run	Slitting Setup
Direct:			
Labor	22.50%	30.00%	25.00%
Supplies	19.20	3.36	10.24
Total	41.70%	33.36%	35.24%
Support:			
Supervisory	6.30%	8.40%	35.00%
Rent	8.00	17.28	14.72
Utilities	10.00	14.16	1.84
Maintenance	14.00	16.00	4.00
Depreciation	20.00	10.80	9.20
Total	58.30%	66.64%	64.76%
TOTAL	100.00%	100.00%	100.00%

As indicated, the relative significance of activity costs within direct activities may vary significantly. These differences are what traditional systems cannot capture.

So far, so good. But how much detail do you want or need? You could break down "process accounts payable" into "batch invoices," "input data," "edit," and "run output," and then further divide "batch invoices" into "sort invoices," "prepare voucher," "run control tape" ad infinitum. But all you've created is a nightmare, not a valid information system!

The answer is that the appropriate level of detail depends on the significance of the activity *in context*. For example, accounts payable processing activities do not usually warrant tracking down to the control tape. An exception might be a service bureau that processes payables for client companies.

RULE OF THUMB: LEVEL OF DETAIL

If an activity makes up less than one or 2 percent of the total for the reporting unit, combine it with other similar activities for purposes of cost application and analysis. The idea is to reduce complexity to the lowest acceptable level, while retaining realism. Otherwise, you risk getting lost in details that do not affect results significantly.

Activity Drivers

What drives costs in your operation? The answer to this question is the key to managing costs.

Activity drivers describe how activities consume resources. As explained in Chapter 1, they are the *quantitative* factors that best represent the causes of costs. For the activity of "process accounts payable," *number of* vendor invoices, checks, vouchers, batches, or other measures may work well. For most companies, the cost differences implicit in using these different bases are insignificant.

For Coil Finishing Co., activity drivers for direct activities include number of rolling passes, slitting setups, and slitting footage. For support activities, the company would use a different set of drivers.

Resource Usage Path

A **resource usage path** (see Exhibit 2-3) is nothing more than a diagram of how activity drivers cause the activities that consume resources. The path starts with the assignment of support activities to direct activities. In Exhibit 2-3, supervision is based on number of setups and labor, occupancy on square footage, maintenance on direct charges of time and material, and so on.

Cost-Cause Grid

By removing a set of activity drivers and activities from the resource usage path, you will have a **cost-cause grid,** giving you cost management for a particular category of activities in a nutshell.

Cost per Unit of Activity Driver

Cost per unit of activity driver is an essential statistic that makes the information usable in all areas, from cost estimating to budgeting. It is determined by dividing costs of an activity ("process accounts payable") by the quantity of activity drivers ("vouchers"). If it costs $50,000 to produce 100,000 vouchers, the cost per voucher is $.50.

The amounts derived for Coil Finishing Co. in Exhibit 2-1 are examples of these statistics.

Exhibit 2-3. Preliminary Resource Usage Path: Coil Finishing Co.

Level I Drivers	Support Activities	Level II Drivers	Operating Activities	Costs
◆ Setups, labor time ◆ Direct charge ◆ Square footage ◆ Direct charge ◆ Value, remaining life ◆ Direct charge, square footage	**Support** Supervision Payroll fringe Occupancy Maintenance Depreciation Utilities	◆ Cold rolling passes ◆ Lineal footage slit ◆ Slitting setups	**Direct** Cold rolling Slitting run Slitting setup	**Resource Usage** End products Inventories Cost of sales Operating expenses

At the heart of ABM design is the resource usage path. A more detailed version is provided in Chapter 3.

Budgets

Exhibit 1-1 and its narrative show how *not* to use budgeting. Budgets do have legitimate uses, however. They are an essential part of planning, and planning is as basic to business as profit. Even the businesses of childhood, from door-to-door sales to lemonade stands, show rudimentary elements of planning. They require recognition of demand, price, and target profit, at least informally. You have to set a price where you can expect a reasonable level of volume, as balanced against the profit earned. You don't need an economics degree to see that charging $100 per cup for lemonade, while it would be extremely profitable, would not generate sufficient demand.

Because real business situations are seldom so simple, planning is correspondingly more formal, ranging up to a strategic plan supported by pages and pages of detail. Throughout, the role of budgeting is crucial: It translates goals, representing the critical problems faced by managers, into measurable targets, which are then implemented to ensure that company divisions work in harmony and attain company goals. An ongoing monitoring of actual performance compared to budget is basic to control of operations. This periodic feedback prompts investigation to show why that actual performance and budget differ.

Let's say you want to introduce a new product line or division. Crucial to the decision of whether to go ahead is the availability of capital to support the operation in its first years. In judging viability, you budget sales, then production and purchases, and target inventory levels. An operating expense budget covers remaining expenses, and a capital expenditure budget includes anticipated investment in property and equipment. These budgets provide a picture, albeit broad, of the financial impact of the proposal so that you can plan for additional financial resources ahead of time, instead of when it's too late.

Failure to plan results in a crisis management mentality where everyone attempts to respond to the seemingly constant boom and bust cycles encountered daily. No matter how hard you try, you cannot break the cycle. While such a chronically reactive strategy is partly self-created, it also arises from the failure of traditional budgeting models to provide the information managers need. The more accurate tool of ABM offers better potential for curing the problem.

Flexible Budgets

Business objectives, technologies, and markets change. To manage costs effectively in new circumstances, your budget tool must be able to adapt to these changes. Although it can be put to the same uses as a conventional budget, the ABM budget is not a conventional budget as you might picture it but one that represents constantly evolving descriptions of cost behavior. A **flexible budget** allows budgeted amounts to vary according to the quantity of underlying drivers. Activity-based management defines the universe of these relationships through this type of budget.

The flexible budget is ABM's method of periodic revalidation. The figures used come from extending the cost per unit of activity driver by the driver quantities for a given period. Either count the actual driver quantities or derive their totals through a simple spreadsheet that explodes end items through bills of activity, as explained in Chapter 3.

You should compare the flexible budget with actual cost data every month to make sure that costs are in line. A flexible budget for Coil Finishing Co. is shown in Exhibit 2-4. If costs show a large variance—say, over 10 percent—look for additional drivers.

Deriving the Sample ABM Model

The Basic Approach

Recall the statistics from Coil Finishing Co. given at the beginning of this chapter:

Activity ("Cost")	Driver ("Cause")	Cost per Driver
Cold rolling	Rolling passes	16.00
Slitting setup	Slitting setups	31.00
Slitting run	Slitting footage	.017

Building on the Coil Finishing Co. example, let's see where the numbers came from. Look at the level I and level II assignments in Exhibit 2-5. Recall that level I is for assigning support activity costs to direct activities and that level II is for assigning direct costs to products.

Let's begin with support activities, and analyze each in turn:

- *Supervision.* Supervision includes the salaries of the supervisor and assistant supervisor, both of whom spend approximately half of their time performing certain parts of slitting setup. The rest of the time is spent in general supervision. Total costs of $140,000 are charged to the three direct activities reflecting these assumptions: Half are assigned to setups, and the other half to direct labor time.

Exhibit 2-4. Flexible Budget: Coil Finishing Co.

Activity	Driver Rate	Driver Quantity	Flexible Budget	Actual Results
Cold rolling	16.00	2,600	$41,600	$40,000
Slitting setup	31.00	510	15,810	16,000
Slitting run	0.017	1,330,000	22,610	22,000
Total			$80,020	$78,000
Percentage variance				2.6%

Based on flexible budget results, the ABM model for Coil Finishing Co. appears to be in control and usable for estimating costs, cost management, efficiency evaluation, and numerous other applications to be described in later chapters.

- *Rent.* Rent is divided between the rolling and slitting operations on the basis of square footage. The slitting portion is further subdivided into run and setup by hours spent on each activity.
- *Utilities.* The 30 percent of utility costs relates to occupancy and is assigned the same way rent is. The remaining 70 percent relates to equipment, and costs are directly charged to activities based on consumption.
- *Maintenance.* Maintenance is directly charged to activities based on consumption.
- *Depreciation.* Finally, depreciation is assigned according to the relative value and remaining useful life of the equipment used in the activities. A subassignment between slitting run and setup is based on time. Assignment of costs in this manner is intended to eliminate the problem of fully depreciated equipment or other unrealistic subsidies.

Level II assignments are as follows:

1. *Direct labor.* The $250,000 costs are assigned according to time spent in each activity.
2. *Supplies.* As with labor, direct charge is used.

(text continues on page 28)

Exhibit 2-5. Detailed Cost Assignments: Coil Finishing Co.

Activity	Activity Driver	Total Drivers	Total Cost	Cold Rolling Drivers	Cold Rolling Cost	Slitting Run Drivers	Slitting Run Cost	Slitting Setup Drivers	Slitting Setup Cost
Support activities:									
Supervisory, 50%	Setups (direct charge)	8,065	$ 60,000					8,065	$ 60,000
Supervisory, 50%	Direct labor time	15,000	60,000	6,750	$ 27,000	4,500	$ 18,000	3,750	15,000
Fringe, 50%	Setups (direct charge)	8,065	10,000					8,065	10,000
Fringe, 50%	Direct labor time	15,000	10,000	6,750	4,500	4,500	3,000	3,750	2,500
Subtotal			$ 140,000		$ 31,500		$ 21,000		$ 87,500
Rent	Square footage	7,500	120,000	2,500	40,000	2,700	43,200	2,300	36,800
Utilities, 30%	Square footage	7,500	15,000	2,500	5,000	2,700	5,400	2,300	4,600
Utilities, 70%	Direct charge	N/A	75,000	N/A	45,000	N/A	30,000		
Subtotal			$ 90,000		$ 50,000		$ 35,400		$ 4,600
Outside maintenance	Direct charge	N/A	$ 120,000	N/A	$ 70,000	N/A	$ 40,000	N/A	$ 10,000
Depreciation	Value/years of life	180,000	150,000	120,000	100,000	32,400	27,000	27,600	23,000
TOTAL SUPPORT			$ 620,000		$ 291,500		$ 166,600		$161,900

Direct activities:

		Direct labor time / Direct charge						
Direct labor	Direct labor time	15,000	6,750		4,500		3,750	
	Direct charge	$ 200,000	$ 90,000		$ 60,000		$ 50,000	
Fringe	Direct charge	N/A	N/A		N/A		N/A	
		50,000	22,500		15,000		12,500	
Subtotal		$ 250,000	$112,500		$ 75,000		$ 62,500	
Supplies	Direct charge	N/A	N/A		N/A		N/A	
		130,000	96,000		8,400		25,600	
Subtotal		$ 130,000	$ 96,000		$ 8,400		$ 25,600	
TOTAL DIRECT		$ 380,000	$208,500		$ 83,400		$ 88,100	
Total costs		$1,000,000	$500,000		$ 250,000		$250,000	
Driver quantities			31,250		15,000,000		8,065	
COST PER DRIVER UNIT			$ 16.00		$ 0.017		$ 31.00	

This diagram illustrates the mechanics involved in level I and level II cost assignments. At each level, cost assignments follow the activity's consumption of activity drivers.

These last two costs combined with the support activity costs deter-mine costing rates. While the example and related exhibit may seem com-plex at first, take a few minutes to walk through it. Based on the descrip-tions above, the cost assignments follow logically.

Exhibit 2-5 is somewhat oversimplified, but you can already begin to see the improvement in management information. This information is the same as that used in Exhibits 1-1 through 1-6. Further refinements will be made in Chapter 3.

Implementing ABM

As with any major system change, ABM requires the full support of man-agement. It involves more than just accounting or estimating; time, energy, and resources are needed to see the change through. Because ABM is grounded in an understanding of costs, input from those actually per-forming or supervising activities is essential to success.

Who's Responsible?

To avoid finger pointing about who bears responsibility for problems, only one individual should be in charge of the implementation. This individual is responsible for developing a detailed plan of implementation, running progress meetings, and making sure that the project is proceeding prop-erly. He or she should also be highly conversant with operations. The proj-ect head need not be an accountant, but he or she must be able to bring about communication between all functions.

ABM's ideal champion is someone who has been burned by a bad system, which in turn has led to a bad decision—be it product, customer, incentive system, or operation. He or she must be eager for the improved information that will come out of an ABM system, since that person knows that better information leads to better decisions—and ultimately to higher profits.

Reducing Duplication of Effort

But you may have difficulty finding the ideal leader for ABM implementa-tion. If your organization is like most, the functions of costing described in this book either are being performed by diverse individuals using their own data systems or are not being performed at all. The data systems themselves are limited by traditional thinking, such as that direct labor drives overhead. Examples of these cost subsystems are as follows:

Use	Data Maintained By:
Financial information	Accounting
Cost estimating, quoting	Sales
Production data	Operations
Budgeting	Planning
Variance analysis	Cost accounting
Management analyses	Special projects

Because these subsystems are usually not routinely reconciled with financial results, they tend to exist in a vacuum. It is doubtful that many could be described as any better than guesstimates of the true information.

ABM brings about immediate efficiency by reducing the duplication of effort involved in maintaining multiple systems. Everyone works with one right answer, instead of several incorrect or incomplete ones. This use of common information should naturally lead to a companywide focus and communication about what's important.

Cooperation

Key to the success of the process is the cooperation of those in operations as well as those in management. Activity drivers are objective factors quantified to achieve an understanding of operations, not to force adherence. To the extent actual results deviate, you should identify additional drivers. The result should be a model that everyone can be comfortable with—and one that will provide understanding, the critical first step toward cost control.

Practical Pointers

Using this type of model will place your company light years ahead of companies using more traditional systems. Certain refinements should be considered, however, as will be discussed in Chapter 3. These include:

- *Customer costs.* Certain customers may have unique requirements that are not reflected in the costing model. For an accurate determination of profitability, it is essential that you capture these costs.

- *Capacity costs.* As you'll recall from Chapter 1, additional costs result when capacity does not match load or demands placed on resources. These must be distinguished for accurate costing.
- *Discretionary costs.* Certain costs are not caused by operations, but by management's discretion. ABM allows you to highlight them.
- *Other types of costs.* The model, as so far shown in this chapter, is limited in usefulness because of its narrow focus on operations. In reality, administrative, selling, and other functions can be highly significant, as will be discussed in Chapter 3.

Finally, because people are most important:

- *Involve everyone.* Without support, ABM is doomed to fail.
- *Understand the sources of resistance.* More to come in Chapter 3.

3

Completing the Picture: The Five Steps in Designing and Implementing an ABM Model

The cost tools described in Chapter 2, while giving you an idea of what ABM entails, were not presented as a complete picture. To keep the explanation simple, certain aspects affecting the process were intentionally left out. Now it's time to consider them. They are incorporated in the more complete resource usage path for Coil Finishing Co. shown in Exhibit 3-1. Notice the addition of discretionary and special requirement categories of operating activities, as well as other refinements.

Adding Reality to the Model

Inequality of Operations

When operations differ so much that distinguishing another activity is justified, do so. Our Coil Finishing Co. model assumes that all operations within the rolling and slitting activities are equal. But suppose a slitting line has a turret that allows the next run to be set up while the current one is running. Then setup time becomes merely a fraction of the conventional way. And if there are differing costs, operations, or capabilities, a single activity is not sufficient to take them all into account.

Or suppose some of the machines are computer-numeric-controlled, meaning preprogrammed setups, so that setup time is reduced to almost zero. Again, the substantial difference in setup cost probably justifies defining a separate activity.

Exhibit 3-1. Resource Usage Path: Coil Finishing Co.

Level I Drivers	Support Activities	Level II Drivers	Operating Activities		Costs
	Support		**Discretionary**		**Resource Usage**
◆ Setups, labor time	Supervision	◆ Discretionary	Capacity decisions		Inventories
◆ Direct charge	Payroll fringe		Abnormal scrap,		Costs of sales
◆ Square footage	Occupancy		rework		Operating expenses
◆ Direct charge	Maintenance		Marketing		
◆ Value, remaining life	Depreciation		Systems development		
◆ Direct charge,	Utilities		Nonmarket costs		
square footage			Cost of capital		
◆ Related transactions	Other administrative				
			Direct		
		◆ Cold rolling passes	Cold rolling		
		◆ Lineal footage slit	Slitting run		
		◆ Slitting setups	Slitting setup		
			Special Requirements		
		◆ Specific customers,	Abnormal scrap,		
		orders, products	rework		
			Expediting		
			Non-normal tolerance		
			Special packaging		
			Special terms		
			Miscellaneous services		

Capacity Decisions and Rework Costs

While our model assumes a normal chargeable level of activity, in reality it may be lower. Let's say that one of the machines is dedicated to specialized work and runs only 30 percent of the time. Does it make sense to fully burden the cost of output of that one machine? At a logical extreme, product costs would become a function of how much utilization there was on a given day. (This topic is more fully covered on page 44.)

On the other hand, when a machine must be so utilized as to incur overtime, again costs become unpredictable. The ABM idea is to segregate these nonproduct costs in reporting and costing so as not to distort decisions for which they are irrelevant.

Discretionary Costs

Let's replace the supervisor with an owner-manager, whose salary and draws vary substantially from year to year depending on the company's performance. The amount may be as little as $10,000 and as much as $500,000. Does it make sense to charge either amount to the cost of the operation?

This type of cost is known as a **discretionary cost.** A discretionary cost is one that cannot be meaningfully related to an activity driver because it is judgmentally determined.

Examples abound of other costs that may be so classified, depending on the nature of the operation and management preference, e.g., stockholder distributions or officers' salaries, an increase in advertising to generate more sales, or employee turnover that requires training time and additional supervision.

Other Direct Costs

Some direct activities extend beyond the operation at hand. For example:

♦ *Administrative activities.* The supervisor may also process documents relating to receipt of customer material and shipment, including invoices. For the sake of simplicity, these are defined in our model as lot-based and charged according to the number of setups. But separating out these costs may help to target areas for improvement.

♦ *Customer requirements.* Some customers may require much more service than others. If most of their orders are produced on machine number 2, should the costs for these orders be charged to that machine? Obviously not: They have nothing to do with the machine or center used; they relate to the customer. Some costs can be logically categorized only as attributable to a customer.

Take customer service activities such as handling complaints. Here again, the number of complaints may be an appropriate driver.

◆ *Product or service line costs.* Costs such as those for research and development may be incurred in developing new products. Or distinct lines of business may be associated with their own management teams. Again, it would be a mistake to associate these costs with a particular direct center or machine, particularly if more than one product line can be routed through it.

Special Requirements Activities

There are often certain activities that are not part of normal costing routines, so a **special requirements** category is intended for tracking them.

Special customer costs may be incurred that are not part of the normal costing model. The difference between the treatment of these costs and those mentioned earlier is that they have not been built into the model. For example, certain customers may require expediting, which causes overtime, or they may have special packaging requirements.

If the supervisor spends 10 percent of his time tracking down orders for these customers, that 10 percent should probably become a special requirements activity.

Inability to Directly Charge

In a way, our model is too perfect—in that such a high portion of support activity costs can be directly charged. The real world often requires that charges draw on activity drivers. In such cases, the most appropriate driver for these costs should be selected.

Now, we turn to the mechanics of building an ABM system. Once you understand them, you'll be able to attain the benefits discussed in subsequent chapters. This chapter discusses the five steps to ABM, but first, some description of elements that characterize operations may be helpful.

The Nature of Operations

Project vs. Continuous Environments

Consider discrete projects, such as shipbuilding, at one extreme and continuous manufacturing, such as oil refining, at the other. Between these extremes fall job shops, batch production, and assembly lines. Many issues of significance in costing vary nearly on a continuum from one extreme to the other. For example:

♦ *The nature of production.* Projects are unique items built to order, whereas continuous production is generally of commodity or stocked items. Product mix in terms of possible options is broadest for the project manufacturer and narrowest for the manager in continuous environments. Detailed scheduling is called for in the former, but not in the latter.

♦ *Labor.* In project environments, the division of labor is undefined. Workers must possess multiple skills, for which they receive relatively high compensation. But in continuous environments, the position of direct labor is so narrowly defined that skill requirements are low and labor can be replaced by automation; labor intensity and compensation are therefore correspondingly less. Project managers are naturally much more concerned with labor than are managers in continuous environments. Therefore, detailed labor reporting is more relevant. In continuous monitoring, the operating flow is more important.

♦ *Machinery.* Like labor, machinery in project or job environments must be able to perform a variety of tasks. General-purpose machines fill these functions. A significant cost of such machines is in setup for a particular use or specification. Utilization may vary. On the other end of the continuum, machinery that is completely dedicated to a particular product or task makes setup altogether unnecessary. The tendency of continuous manufacturers to be more capital-intensive makes machine utilization a top issue.

♦ *Inventories.* These also reflect the nature of the operation. For custom orders, or projects, raw materials are usually purchased after orders have been obtained, whereas in continuous manufacturing, they are stocked. Work-in-process is large in the former but small in the latter. Finished goods for projects are nonexistent, whereas they predominate in manufacturing to stock.

You can extend this analysis to any type of operation. Service companies (such as professional firms) and the construction industry have much in common with project manufacturers: They tend to utilize highly skilled labor, and most of these organizations are people-intensive. Similarly, the work flow in more standardized services (such as those for banking customers) may resemble a batch manufacturing process.

Cost Implications

From the characteristics covered here, certain cost implications are evident.

Project environments would be compatible with detailed labor analysis, labor-paced operation drivers, high lot-based costs, high handling costs, many variable directly charged costs, and diverse bases for overhead. Because direct labor is such a large portion of total costs, these companies may utilize time reporting for direct charges to job costs; time may even be the basis for billing customers. From an equipment perspective, rate normalization and setup are important factors to consider.

One conflict for ABM in a project environment is whether, because of the intense variety of work, time is an appropriate base to use for applying costs. Because of the large portion of total costs represented by skilled labor, time may indeed be acceptable. But it should be noted that improvements in estimating and other information can come about from the use of activity drivers.

Another potential problem is the effect of multiskilled personnel on costing rates. Crossover of workers between departments may be frequent. Optimally, costing should reflect an individual's actual labor rate no matter where he or she is working. But while this is easy to implement in union settings where pay scales are known to all, in others there may be a need to compromise by using departmental average rates.

Continuous environments tend toward line- or machine-paced operations, high overhead costs, potentially complex joint product allocations, and high fixed costs. Invested capital is dedicated to production of specific products, with changeover seldom if ever. Because price is market-driven, the key to survival is reducing costs through economies of scale or technology. In commodity production, operations are so highly standardized that the cost of labor becomes insignificant.

Batch and repetitive or line environments fall between the extremes of job-shop customization and continuous process standardization. As such, many of the entities in this classification are actually hybrids of job and process manufacturing. Product design may become increasingly standardized. Production may be to stock as well as to order. Finished goods and raw materials may emerge as inventory components.

The equipment in batch or repetitive environments is more likely to be dedicated to certain tasks or operations. Capital intensity is increased over job shops. Lot sizes tend to be larger, and setups less significant. Correspondingly, skilled labor is less necessary and becomes a smaller element in cost control.

Sample systems, with some nonmanufacturing examples, dealing with the issues raised here will be discussed in Chapter 4. For now, consider where your operation falls on this spectrum. This will shed light on what's important in costing. Let's get specific.

The Five Steps to ABM

Having covered some of the complexities involved in adding realism, we turn next to the five steps needed to build an ABM model. They are as follows:

1. Develop a resource usage path.
2. Assign costs, level I.
3. Assign costs, level II.
4. Budget drivers and relate to costs.
5. Validate the model.

Developing a Resource Usage Path

After considering where your operation falls on the continuum, your first step is to facilitate organization of cost information by mapping out direct activities. The tool for doing this is the **resource usage path** (as introduced in Chapter 2 and refined here).

The resource usage path provides a common framework for analyzing ABM systems for a diversity of industries. It is the essence of ABM and answers the question of what causes costs, i.e., of how resources are consumed. The resource usage path (see Exhibit 3-2 for a generic example) is the ABM blueprint for your organization. It can be applied to practically any industry, and you will benefit by investing some time in learning its structure.

Referring to the exhibit, notice the sections provided in Sample Co.'s path:

- ◆ Support activities
- ◆ Operating activities

Exhibit 3-2. Resource Usage Path: Sample Co.

Level I Drivers	Support Activities	Level II Drivers	Operating Activities	Costs
♦ Direct charge is best ♦ Time, head count ♦ Square footage ♦ Head count ♦ Time and materials ♦ Vendors, P/Os ♦ Parts ♦ Asset value ♦ Value, remaining life ♦ Quantity consumed ♦ Head count, payroll dollars ♦ Related transactions	**Support** General activities Supervision Occupancy Personnel Maintenance Purchasing Stockeeping Asset-carrying costs Depreciation Utilities Payroll fringe Other administrative	♦ Discretionary ♦ Cold rolling passes ♦ Lineal footage slit ♦ Slitting setups ♦ Specific customers, orders, products	**Discretionary** Capacity decisions, bottlenecks Abnormal scrap, rework Marketing Systems development Non-market costs Cost of capital **Direct** Unit activities Transaction activities Lot–based activities Customer activities Order activities Service or product-line activities Expected scrap, rework **Special Requirements** Abnormal scrap, rework Expediting Non-normal tolerance Special packaging Special terms Miscellaneous services	**Resource Usage** End products/services Inventories Cost of sales Operating expenses

Within operating activities are the following additional categories:

- ◆ Direct activities
- ◆ Discretionary activities
- ◆ Special requirements activities

The significance of these categories will become clearer as this book progresses. At one extreme are the management-determined discretionary expenditures; at the other, the special requirements, or customer-determined costs. The discretionary category of capacity decisions, for example, has a big role in dealing with efficiency, as discussed further in Chapter 5.

Let's look at each category in more detail.

Support Activities   Support activities are those that are consumed by more than one operating activity. As indicated in Chapter 2, the idea behind level I assignment is to create a basis for organizing information. Support services are charged to operating activities at level I, and at level II, are analyzed with respect to end products or services, as opposed to the more traditional allocation over departments.

Unless you keep highly detailed records, assignment to direct activities must use activity drivers. Maintenance and supervision, for example, should be charged, on the basis of work orders or best estimates, to those activities consuming them; personnel costs, assigned according to head counts in the various direct activities; occupancy costs, driven by square footage occupied; procurement costs, based on purchase orders related to each center.

Operating Activities   Operating activities are the end activities performed by the organization in providing products or services to customers. They include discretionary, direct, and special requirements activities.

Direct Activities   Direct activities are those driven by activity drivers in providing end-chargeable outputs. Within each operation, certain activities may be distinguished, including material handling, setup, and run. Drivers for these activities are also defined. If an activity appears to have more than one driver, perhaps an additional activity needs to be defined. If you refer back to Exhibit 2-3, you will see that for Coil Finishing Co., the direct activities found in manufacturing operations are slitting and cold rolling. Within slitting, setup is distinguished from run. Depending on their significance, activities can be delineated further or combined with others.

While it is not as easy to generalize for service operations, a rule of thumb is that direct activities should cover the services performed. Loan servicing activities, for example, include transaction processing, lender reporting, compliance, analysis, and inspection. (See Chapter 4 for in-depth examples from several service industries.)

Discretionary Activities **Discretionary activities** are distinguished from activities that are directly attributable to end products or services and customers. They are brought about by management decision, and cannot meaningfully be traced to end items. An example of a discretionary activity is a decision to add or reduce capacity or to work overtime.[1]

The opposite of discretionary is **chargeable.** The following case should make the concept clearer.

PLASTICS MANUFACTURER

Plastics Manufacturer has two molding lines in which it runs plastic containers of varying colors. Its cost system includes only run time; setup is treated as overhead and averaged over direct labor time. Thus the costs for the two lines appear identical. In reality, however, black causes setup time to double because of the need to purge dark colors. Management knows the costs are questionable, and turns to ABM.

Result: Under ABM, the setup cost is properly treated as chargeable. If the dark product is not run, the purging cost does not occur. Treating setup as chargeable gives management control over the costs.

Special Requirements Activities   At the other end of the continuum are special requirements activities. These are activities that cannot be captured as direct or discretionary; rather, they are determined by customers' needs. Examples include special terms or overtime incurred for certain customers. Should these requirements become routine, they would evolve into direct activities over time.

The resource usage path provides a costing blueprint that connects support and operating activities to their activity drivers. It allows you to focus on what matters.

Assigning Level I Costs

While it would be nice if constructing a resource usage path was all there was to designing a system, much essential "dirty work" remains to be

[1] Of course, every decision, including whether or not to remain in business at all, is discretionary in the final analysis. That is not what's intended here, however.

done. Assigning level I costs, i.e., assigning costs to activities, is the first step in getting your hands dirty.

In ABM, *assignment* refers to the fact that costs follow causal relationships; this is in contrast to the arbitrary *allocations* found in traditional costing. A significant way of assigning costs is to use activity drivers, intended to reflect causal relationships between activities and the costs they consume. In costing, activity costs are spread over activity drivers when applying costs. This is not the same as averaging, however.

RULE OF THUMB: AVERAGING VS. ACTIVITY DRIVING

Dividing costs by activity drivers seems like averaging, as, for example, when purchasing costs are averaged over the number of orders to determine an average cost per order. While this makes sense to a degree, it misses the purpose of ABM. If costs per unit of driver are roughly the same, averaging is appropriate; otherwise, you need to identify additional activity drivers to remove the variance. For example, you may have to use setup time instead of number of setups as an activity driver if the variation between types of setups is large. A rule of thumb is that variation within 10 percent or so of an average is acceptable.

The following table summarizes ABM techniques for assigning support activity costs to operating activities:

Technique	Costs
Direct charges of time and materials	Maintenance, supervision, energy, depreciation, indirect labor, inspection, scrap
Square footage	Occupancy costs, including rent, depreciation, building maintenance, utilities, insurance, security
Purchase orders, vendors	Procurement costs
Payroll	Payroll taxes, pension
Head count	Personnel costs, employee medical insurance, plant accounting

You will see from the table that a problem has already surfaced. Maintenance and supervision functions consume employee benefits; occupancy consumes maintenance costs. You must assign costs systematically to ensure proper results.

RULE OF THUMB: ORDER OF ASSIGNMENT AT LEVEL I

Start with the supporting center that affects the largest number of other supporting centers. Employee benefits, maintenance, or occupancy could qualify. Once that center's costs have been fully assigned, move on to the center affecting the next largest number of supporting centers. If crossover is significant, determine those assignments simultaneously—as, for example, where a maintenance department consumes occupancy costs but also contributes to the occupancy cost pool by providing janitorial or grounds services.

Now, let's analyze some of the major categories of support activities.

Supervision   Supervision time varies according to operating activities. It is preferable to charge these costs directly. The next step, as covered at level II, is to determine the character of these costs. For each operation, you should analyze supervision further. Supervision of an assembly operation may vary according to complexity of the items being assembled; in very complex situations, the *number* of components may be an adequate activity driver. Supervision in other operations may require inspection of a setup prior to beginning the run; those supervision costs are related to the setup activity for assignment to products over the number of setups. Other supervision costs, such as those relating to order-type activities or customer special requirements, should be charged appropriately.

Quality Control and Inspection   Quality control and inspection costs also may entail many activities caused by different activity drivers. Once these costs are assigned to direct activities, analysis should begin. Variability in output of manual operations compared to automated ones may drive inspection. Or customers may need products that meet special tolerances or exacting specifications. In that case, inspection for these products should be charged directly to those items.

Maintenance   Maintenance should be charged directly to operating activities. Automated operations tend to need more maintenance than manual ones. In companies with sophisticated maintenance programs in place, activity drivers may already be available. Certain tasks may be routinized to occur after a customary amount of operating hours, just as automobiles are set to be tuned up after a certain number of miles. Maintenance requirements for overhead cranes may be based on the number or weight of lifts. Unplanned maintenance costs incurred in reaction to breakdowns may be appropriately driven by the number of occurrences.

Depreciation In many companies, depreciation amounts are so distorted by tax laws that they are not meaningful for costing. Most pieces of equipment are fully depreciated long before their life is over. For that reason, depreciation based on tax methods should be discarded in favor of using an estimated replacement value for cost—usually available from reports prepared for property insurance purposes. To this information, a true remaining useful life may be applied. The calculated depreciation is directly charged to the appropriate direct cost center and, as will be described later, assigned to products using a normalized activity driver base.

Employee Benefits Employee benefits requires additional explanation. While they are assigned by direct charge, the process is usually more complex than it may appear. Benefits must be related to all activities that consume them, including supporting, customer, product-line, and discretionary activities. In addition, some of these costs may vary with head count, hours, or employee turnover instead of simply by payroll dollars. View such costs as follows:

Technique	Costs
Payroll dollars, less overtime premium	FICA taxes, workers' compensation insurance
Head count	Medical insurance, unemployment taxes, paid absences
Hours	Pension, as applicable
Employee turnover	Hiring, training, uniforms
Overtime premium	Incremental FICA taxes

Payroll dollars less overtime premium are adequate for assigning FICA taxes and workers' compensation insurance, because that base reflects the relationship of these costs. For salaries exceeding FICA limits, assignment would ideally be adjusted.

Gross head count is appropriate for medical insurance, unemployment taxes, and paid absences. Depending on company policy, full-time head count may be more appropriate for medical insurance and paid absences. Because the taxable wage limits are low, head count also tends to be a better driver for unemployment taxes than gross pay or some other measure.

Some pension contributions relate directly to hours worked. In those cases, hours is the appropriate base. Indicators of employee turnover may best relate to new employee costs, including hiring, training, and uniforms. Finally, overtime should be burdened only with the true incremental costs it causes, such as additional FICA.

While for budgeting purposes the technique indicated would be used, for costing you can add benefits to a base hourly rate, as long as they are separately identified. Taking total benefits in percentage relation to total payroll may provide an acceptable shortcut if payroll is relatively insignificant.

Occupancy   Few topics cause more controversy in costing than occupancy costs. Because rent or building depreciation is unrelated to volume, the question becomes whether it is meaningful to apply either at the product level. If excess space is made available, it might be subleased to another company. While the choice of including occupancy costs is up to you, the "fixed" nature of these costs should be highlighted. One solution for fixed costs is normalization, discussed in the next section.

Fixed Costs   Certain support costs, like rent and depreciation, do not vary with activity levels. How can costing properly reflect this? One alternative is to exclude fixed costs altogether from short-term decisions, as if they did not exist. At the opposite extreme, fixed costs can be fully absorbed in all operations, regardless of volume level. It is argued that even if only one unit goes through the metal shop area, all costs in that area must be absorbed by that unit.

A legitimate compromise between these extremes is the idea of **normalization,** which applies the ABM principle of segregating unutilized capacity. The budget base for applying fixed costs is adjusted to reflect a normal level of activity or capacity. This prevents underutilized operations from being overburdened when being considered in cost estimating or other applications. The underapplied fixed overhead represents idle capacity or volume variance.

In addition, once you assume normal capacity, a measure of the fixed costs at that volume level is available. This can be used in marketing decisions. An operation with substantial excess capacity may offer its salespeople more discretion in reducing prices to some level above variable costs. Normal capacity or higher would justify full-absorption costing plus markup.

What you need is a **normal fixed costing rate** for use in cost estimating, with monthly comparison to actual costs. The difference is idle capacity, which you can highlight in reporting, along with downtime, as a discretionary expense.

To illustrate the disposition of actual from normal, here is a further example from our model.

COIL FINISHING CO.

One of Coil Finishing Co.'s slitting lines, machine C, is newly installed and has not been fully utilized. The derivation of the normal rate is shown in Exhibit 3-3. The budgeted fixed costs related to machine C are divided over footage and setup activity drivers that are adjusted to reflect normal capacity. As illustrated in Exhibit 3-4, the method for detailed costing is normalized in contrast to actual. Applying costs results in a residual idle capacity cost.

Other Categories Numerous other supporting service categories may exist. It is essential for costing that these be related to the drivers most reflective of underlying activities. Costs for administering production may be higher for custom orders or for a bottleneck operation. Other examples are elsewhere in the text. (See especially Chapter 4.)

Assigning Level II Costs

At level II, ABM assigns costs to activities and activities to the most reflective activity drivers. The idea of level II in traditional costing, in contrast, means averaging all costs over direct labor hours or equivalent units.

In ABM, the methods of assigning costs to activities within direct centers are limited only by the designer's creativity. Some possibilities are as follows:

Exhibit 3-3. Calculation of Normalized Rate

CALCULATION FOR MACHINE C.

	Run	Setup
Fixed costs assigned	$6,000	$5,000
Normal capacity:		
Footage	2,000,000	
Setups		1,000
Normalized rate per unit of driver	$.003	$5.00

Normalized rate calculations for fixed costs are based on an assumption of normal capacity. Activity drivers for fixed costs associated with underutilized machinery must be adjusted to reflect a normal capacity level.

Exhibit 3-4. Actual vs. Normal: Coil Finishing Co.

CALCULATION FOR MACHINE C.

Fixed costs applied:

Footage	$1,500,000
Normalized rate	.003
Subtotal	$ 4,500
Setups	750
Normalized rate	$ 5.00
Subtotal	$ 3,750
TOTAL	$ 8,250

Actual fixed costs:

Depreciation	$ 5,000
Occupancy	7,500
Total actual costs	$12,500
Difference: Idle capacity	$ 4,250

This exhibit demonstrates the calculation of idle capacity in machinery for reporting. Idle capacity is the difference between actual costs and fixed costs applied using a normalized rate.

- ◆ Direct charge, the most preferred method
- ◆ Relationships between other costs of the activity, e.g., between payroll and payroll taxes
- ◆ Outputs of the center
- ◆ Estimates, based on interviews with operations personnel
- ◆ Engineered machine standards

With support costs assigned, the next step is to finalize the relationships between activities and activity drivers. Some examples of activity drivers for assigning costs to products are as follows:

Activity	Activity Drivers
Energy	Run time, weight, units
Inspection	Units, complexity
Maintenance	Machine hours, weight processed, scheduled times
Material handling	Weight, distance
Order processing	Orders
Processing	Run time, product design, components assembled, number of operations, weight processed, machine hours
Setup	Setups
Supervision	Time, head count, complexity
Wait, downtime	Changeovers, breakdowns
Warehousing, shipping, packing	Orders, units, weight

Note that this table is not intended to be exhaustive. In assigning level II costs, mirror your operation as closely as possible. Do not allow preconceptions to interfere with making the best possible cost assignments.

Similarly, product-line costs and customer costs should be assigned to the major product lines and customers responsible, respectively. Remaining product-line and customer costs should be assigned reasonably. These costs are kept separate from each other so as not to distort product costs and to allow for their recognition at a meaningful level. In cost estimating, they may be unitized for application to products. For example, the assignment of engineering costs to product lines may be based on the number of change notices. The costs are then translated to the unit level by spreading them over an output measure.

For those costs that do not relate to particular ABM direct activities, you have the options of the discretionary and special requirements classifications. For example, reported downtime and underabsorbed equipment overhead may be discretionary. Separating them from direct activities is important. Unless they are classified outside of direct activities, inefficiencies such as downtime, scrap, rework, and overtime can cause irrelevant cost variations.

You must determine how to classify particular items. Because overtime and rework costs may be chargeable to customers, they may warrant being classified as special requirements rather than as discretionary. Even if you prefer to classify them as product costs, keep them distinct. For example, you may prefer to assign overtime premium costs to products on the basis of total direct labor hours. While acceptable, preferably these costs should be identified separately so as not to factor them in to decisions where they are irrelevant.

Adding detail can remove variation. The more complex the operation, the more detail may be required to adequately reflect its nuances. This does not mean that ABM has to be more complex than a traditional system. ABM should use only what is needed to properly reflect operations.

RULE OF THUMB: COMPLEXITY FACTORS

Complexity factors can better associate activity drivers and activities. For example, in our Coil Finishing Co. model, activity costs are driven by both footage and gauge (required passes) of coiled metal. If this is the case in your operation, you may separate cost per foot by light, medium, and heavy gauge; or, you may use a complexity factor. You can substitute a factor as long as it is explicitly defined and understood by users of the system.

The activities defined should completely account for the costs of the operation. Remember, activities within an operation commonly require different activity drivers, such as run versus setup activities. Refer to Compendium II for pitfalls to avoid in defining activities as you build your model.

With costs assigned, the bulk of your work is complete. At this point, edit the model. Challenge the existence of insignificant activities. Prune excess complexity to where it becomes manageable.

At this time, you may question the way the accounting area has maintained—or failed to maintain—information. Accounting may be slow to adapt its categorizations to new operations or product lines. The designer's creation may call for changes in accounting upon completion. To facilitate future updates, accounting should agree to make the necessary changes.

Budgeting Drivers and Relating Them to Costs

The conventional ABM approach is described next; then an alternative is offered.

The Conventional Approach   After assigning costs, you must budget activity-driver quantities to determine costs per unit of activity driver—an essential statistic.

Usually, ABM practitioners suggest counting actual activity-driver quantities, including the number of orders, distances of materials moved, and types of parts assembled. While cumbersome the first time through, the eventual goal is for ABM users to modify their computer systems to capture the new data.

To make the conventional approach workable, two controls must be in place:

1. *Aggregate vs. detailed comparison.* Activity drivers applied at the product or bill-of-activity level, such as would be used in cost estimating, must be compared with totals used in the system for budgeting.

For example, the total number of purchase orders associated with each product extended by the number of products should be the same as that shown in the budget. Without being able to compare the two, there is no way for you to ensure that the model is valid and up-to-date.

2. *Control over errors.* Errors are common whenever data are first used in a new way for a new purpose. For example, if there is an error in the number of purchase orders obtained by comparing the beginning and ending numbers assigned for the period, it may be that void orders or vendor debit memos have also been included in the sequence.

In practice, there are many compromises, some of them unwise. For example, you may be tempted to substitute activity drivers requiring less effort to accumulate for those that better reflect a causal relationship. Remember, if you do, model quality suffers.

The Automated Approach   Because of the difficulties associated with the conventional ABM implementation, you may want to consider the following automated approach to budgeting activity drivers through bills of activity. You can easily adapt this alternative approach to spreadsheet programs, which greatly eases the complexity and frustration of the more standard implementation just discussed. This approach can derive activity-driver budgets while simultaneously providing estimating formats for detailed costing.

Although requiring nothing more than a full ABM implementation, the automated approach eliminates the data-gathering step. This not only reduces cost but improves system efficiency and quality. It does, however, require a change in mindset. Actual activity-driver data must be replaced with a proper assignment of costs among products.

Your first step is to define your end items, whether products or services, as would be done on a master production schedule. Then determine your end-item quantities, basing them either on budgets or on history. Next, use the end-item information just created to identify the bills of activity needed.

A **bill of activity** is similar to a bill of material. The bill of activity lists activities required to produce a product, the associated activity driver, and the quantity of the activity driver incurred per end item. It is most desirable to list activities in the sequence in which they are performed. Activity drivers come from a variety of sources, e.g., from product characteristics. If significant activities include material handling, slitting, and assembly, the drivers could be product characteristics of weight, length, and number of components assembled, respectively.

Once bills of activities are available, you then use them to explode historical or forecasted end items manufactured, similar to the way in which you would explode a master production schedule into material requirements planning. With this spreadsheet method, the budgeted activity drivers, determined manually in conventional ABM, are generated automatically. At this stage, agreement of budgeted activity drivers with the sum of forecasted item bills of activities is ensured, and the cost of data accumulation drops dramatically.

This simpler and more valid alternative addresses the deficiencies of the conventional approach as follows:

- Because activity-driver budgets can be derived from bills of activity extended at scheduled production, you can select the *best* drivers available, instead of the least expensive ones.
- The ability to calculate driver budgets without data ensures congruity of activity-driver totals with amounts applied to products. In addition, you need no longer be concerned about the potential for errors in accumulating driver data.
- There is no longer any need to modify software in order to capture actual activity-driver data.

Although some might insist on comparing the calculated activity drivers with actual quantities, that not only is unnecessary but leads to inefficiency and detracts from model quality. Once you have the budgeted rates, you can test them easily and frequently by exploding actual end items through bills of activity and comparing the result with actual costs. This essential step in model validation is what old approaches miss.

Models gain accuracy. Unusual drivers may be used, including some that might be difficult to track on an ongoing basis. You can also be sure that budgeted drivers reflect realistic product mixes.

What's lost is a two-way variance analysis, i.e., how much of the difference between budget and actual arises from quantities as opposed to costing rates. A quantity variance cannot occur, however, when costs are driven by product characteristics; for example, the number of components per end item multiplied by the number of end products is the actual driver quantity. Similarly, you can obtain the activity drivers of product weight, length, and volume from end items without worrying about two-way variances.

Where two-way variances may matter is in the other relationships, such as purchase orders to purchasing cost. A product budgeted as requiring three purchase orders may need only two if two items are ordered together, leading to a quantity variance that may cast doubt on model design. In such a case, however, the change in assignment of purchasing cost to products is insignificant. The use of drivers not intended to total an actual amount may even be desirable.

Continuing with the purchasing example, the number of vendors may drive certain purchasing costs, such as vendor relations. One product may need three vendors and another five. But if the two products have vendors in common, a total of eight vendors is incorrect. This type of flexibility would not be possible using conventional ABM.

Moreover, ABM reporting excludes traditional two-way variances. ABM strives to eliminate variances by identifying drivers associated with them. The goal is a cost model based on the understanding of what incurs cost, not traditional "carrot and stick" costing.

Ideally, the bills of activities have multiple levels. A product-level cost is seen as the top level. Then, batch-level costs, such as order and setup drivers, are identified. Finally, end items and their components are structured.

All you need for "explosion" is spreadsheet software available for personal computers. For the sake of simplicity, you can combine complex end products or services at a modular level, as in a two-level master production schedule. In this way, you separate what products or services have in common from the custom finishing touches. End items may be aggregated to a point where assignments will not significantly differ from a more detailed approach.

Automating bills of activity is most beneficial when activity drivers are physical characteristics. Here, you derive activity-driver budgets simply by summing characteristics from an explosion of projected end items. See Exhibit 3-5. Note that the costs are separated into units and

Exhibit 3-5. Bill-of-Activity Approach to Activity-Driver Budgets: Activity-Driver Budget for 1,000 Units of Product A

ACTIVITY-DRIVER CHARACTERISTIC

Unit Costs	Per Item	Per 1,000
Product weight	102 lbs.	102,000 lbs.
Surface area	2,500 in.	2,500,000 in.
Length	37 in.	37,000 in.
Component parts	12 ea.	12,000 ea.
Times handled	7 ea.	7,000 ea.
Lot-based costs (assuming 50 per lot)	Per lot	Per 20 lots
Setups	1 ea.	20 ea.
Purchase orders	5 ea.	100 ea.
Vendors	3 ea.	60 ea.
Other lot costs	Per 5 lots	Per 20 lots
Tooling (change every 5 lots)	1 ea.	4 ea.

A departure from past ABM methods that can improve model efficiency and quality is explosion of a bill of activities through end-item budgets. As illustrated here, this may be done at several stages, including the unit and lot stages.

lots. Whereas the first two vary directly with the number of end items produced, the third requires an assumption as to manufacturing lot size. Additional lot-based costs may require different lot-size assumptions.

Once activity drivers are budgeted, you can relate them to the cost assignments for rates per unit of driver. Costing rates are derived from dividing activity cost by quantities of the associated activity drivers. If the drivers reflect nonnormal activity levels, you should normalize drivers for fixed costs.

You can then apply the costing rates, as desired, to bills of activities for product or service costs. The rates are also available for estimating, hypotheticals, and other decision support activities. The data are versatile and may be used in analyzing profitability by product line, customer, or anything else that's useful.

The automated approach frees up creativity and leads to more efficient, high-quality implementations at lower cost. Everyone benefits.

Validating the Model

Your model must pass the "smell test"; that is, it must make sense to the users. Rates and bases should be flexible in the first months of ABM implementation, until users are reasonably satisfied that the system is realistic. After that, the system should not need frequent updating.

Events that might cause need for change include:

- New labor contracts with pay-rate changes
- The opening of a new facility
- Implementation of new production technology
- Introduction of a new product

Once you have costs per unit of activity driver, tools are available for cost estimating as well as budgeting. The comparison of budget to actual, at both the aggregate budgeting level and the detailed costing level, ensures accuracy on an ongoing basis.

Budgeting in this case consists of the following steps:

1. Where bills of activity are in place, input and explode actual end items into activity-driver totals. If they are not in place, provide for accumulating this information as easily as possible on an interim basis.
2. Apply the budgeted rates per unit of activity driver to the driver quantities. The extension of the two numbers represents the budget for the period and is based on actual driver consumption at budgeted costing rates.
3. Finally, compare the general ledger and budget information. Preferably, the spreadsheet would contain dollar and percentage variance columns. Set tolerances for investigation according to the nature of the item, its significance, and its underlying accounting method.

Comparing actual and budgeted costs can be likened to measuring application of overhead in traditional costing, where actual quantities at budgeted rates are compared to actual costs to determine whether costs are over- or underabsorbed. ABM uses the same approach but in more detail. The application comparison is by line item, rather than overall, to pinpoint sources of differences. The ability to achieve this level of accuracy comes from ABM's realistic, multiple-base approach.

You can use a similar approach in monitoring projects or departmental performance. Once activity costs, drivers, and cost per driver are determined, progress-to-date can be assessed either by comparing actual drivers incurred to quantities budgeted or by calculating budget earned by extending actual drivers at budgeted rates and comparing to actual costs. See Compendium I for more details.

While not necessary, should you choose to integrate ABM with general ledger accounting, the ABM budget also serves to provide the basis for costs applied by operation. For example, costing for a stamping operation would contain a listing of its actual costs for a period. The costs would be applied by crediting departmental costs and debiting finished inventory at the ABM budget amount, equal to actual activity drivers incurred for the period at budgeted rates. This ensures tie-in for inventories costed at these rates.

Under complex systems, costing can proceed by direct center, with costs applied at the difference between costs of input and costs of output based on budgeted rates per activity driver. Costs applied represent a credit for value added, which is compared to actual. The corresponding debit attaches to costs of the related inventory as it moves through stages of completion (see Exhibit 3-6 for an example).

Other Issues

Generally Accepted Accounting Principles

ABM methods are acceptable under generally accepted accounting principles (GAAP) as long as only product costs attach to products. Selling and general and administrative costs must be excluded. While desirable, changing your method of valuing ending inventory may prove difficult. An overall costing of ending inventories is of greater concern to external users than internal. For an ABM system, you need only a way to translate production into consumption of activity-driver resources. The activity drivers extended at budgeted rates are compared to actual costs on a line-by-line basis. This ensures that the model is functioning properly.

If you do choose to change inventory valuation, the inventory system stated in ABM costs must be readily convertible to a GAAP basis for external uses.

Interim Reporting

A common problem for manufacturers is the reporting of financial results at interim periods between physical inventories. At one extreme, you may

Exhibit 3-6. Integrated System Example

Description	Debit	Credit
Inventory account, direct center A:		
Beginning balance	$100,000	
Transfers in	400,000	
Production value added	250,000	
Transfers out		$650,000
Ending balance	$100,000	
Production costs, direct center A:		
Actual costs	$260,000	
Production value added		$250,000
Budget-actual variance		$ 10,000

Under an integrated ABM system, inventories and production would be stated at ABM budget amounts. A budget-actual variance would automatically arise from comparison of actual costs with those applied.

use a single gross profit assumption in determining costs of sales, and with it adjust inventory. At the other extreme, you may integrate perpetual or job cost records with general ledger reporting to ensure congruity of sales, purchases, accounts receivable, accounts payable, and inventories. No matter, there is a distrust of the information because of the errors that may occur.

ABM affords control at interim by providing a budget based on production information, rather than cost of goods sold. As long as production data and costs incurred can be properly cut off, they are comparable to ABM budgets. This allows a level of control at interim that before implementation of ABM may have seemed impossible.

Budget Reporting

Reporting formats may adhere to ABM classifications, or be organized along other lines that you may feel more comfortable with, at least initially. This eases the shock of implementation. For example, if direct labor and repairs represent line items in the desired report, activity drivers associated with deriving these amounts should be determined and totaled appropriately.

Sources of Resistance

As emphasized in Chapter 2, ABM calls for cross-functional cooperation. To achieve this means overcoming potential resistance. Some of the groups from which to expect resistance are covered here.

◆ *Accounting personnel.* How would you like to wake up one morning and be told that your knowledge and experience are obsolete? Many controllers pride themselves on the background and expertise that enabled them to install sophisticated traditional systems in their companies. Telling them they are wrong will naturally lead to vehement refusal, at least initially. Accountants must be prepared to accept that the old way is no longer the right one. Only then can they be trusted to give honest effort in ABM implementation.

◆ *Estimators and approvers.* The "judgment" that was once the domain only of the initiated is now expected of all. Decisions that were made in a hidden world may be open to question. Estimators and approvers may perceive this opening up as a loss of authority and may be insulted at being required to enumerate and document the process. Documentation must back decisions as never before. You must be able to convince these threatened individuals of the improvements that ABM will bring about. It can be sold as a sharing of information once restricted to estimating with the rest of the company so that it may be factored in to strategic and other decisions appropriately.

◆ *Operations.* Operations people are so used to getting the short end of the information stick that they are likely to distrust those involved in ABM implementation. The distrust of the old system is likely to carry over to the new system, unless an effort is made to ensure their involvement. As a major user of information from the system, operations must be heavily involved in designing the system if the system is to be successful.

◆ *Line managers and salespeople.* The behavior of line managers and salespeople has been very much influenced by old incentive compensation methods. Line managers have learned that building inventory could camouflage a bad month, and salespeople have learned that custom or difficult work is very easy to get under the old pricing formula. Now that they've mastered the rules to the old game, a new, less manipulable version is being introduced. Naturally, this creates tension. However, once they realize that ABM is based on cost understanding rather than regulation, the game component should disappear. Without the need to satisfy the peculiarities of a certain game, their performance loses constraints to its improvement.

◆ *Those who contributed to the inefficiency.* No one likes to admit that they're wrong. Employees who are sensitive to criticism may interpret the situation as if they themselves were to blame, regardless of the facts. Conscientious employees may sense that the inefficiency that led to the implementation of the new system reflects on them. It is natural for them to be guilt-ridden and defensive. Reassuring them that the culprit is impersonal should mitigate the problem.

◆ *General inertia.* Even upper management may fall victim to inertia. When presented with information showing that what was thought to be a prized product line has actually been generating losses, the immediate reaction is disbelief coupled with a tendency to distrust what's new. The need to overcome denial of challenges to the old mindset is essential to moving forward.

The common stake in the present system is not having to change. Change, in the minds of many, is equivalent to an admission of wrongdoing. Because many will refuse to admit that misinformation or inefficiency exists, it may take the opinion of an outside expert to awaken some to the reality of the situation.

As suggested in Chapter 1, you should depersonalize the issues. The problem is not with any particular person but with the activity drivers creating the inefficiency.

Overcoming Barriers

Many of the barriers to implementing ABM take the form of various criticisms that will be discussed here. Major arguments against ABM include its complexity, cost orientation, lack of new information, departure from accounting standards, and radical nature.

Complexity

When first presented, ABM may appear to be more unmanageable and complex than traditional systems.

"The Old System Is Simpler."   Even in the face of today's computers, many still argue against cost system improvement on the basis of complexity. But there is no predefined complexity level that a system must meet in order to be called ABM. Systems can be as simple or as complex as their users desire. Any recognition of underlying operations in costing would be an improvement over most systems.

"Too Much Data."   As touched on previously, the approach of conventional ABM to budgeting activity drivers by counting is problematic and costly. Because the driver budgets and detailed product costs are generated separately, reconciliation, if even attempted, may prove difficult or require budget revision. Without the ability to readily test actual unit-driver quantities at budgeted rates against actual costs through flexible budgeting, assurance of the accuracy of the cost model is in doubt. The solution presented is to use budgeted end items and bills of activity to explode out activity-driver budgets, making reconciliation automatic.

"Costly Reprogramming Is Needed."   A common source of resistance is the perceived level of software modification required to support the activity-driver budgeting system. Software, however, need not be modified to capture driver data if such data are derived through an explosion of end items through bills of activity.

"It Departs From Accounting Standards."   As already discussed, with today's technology, the departure of ABM from accounting standards should not be a barrier to implementation. GAAP should be complied with by using the simplest methods possible. A costing of equivalent units, for example, can even be performed on a nonintegrated spreadsheet, which is usually all that external auditors or others will require.

Cost Orientation

The arguments criticizing ABM as too cost-oriented amount to general ones against cost system information.

"Choice of System Won't Make Much of a Difference."   Usually, arguments that ABM won't make a difference are arguments against cost systems in general. People espousing this viewpoint claim that businesses are run by the seat of the pants and information doesn't matter. The many examples of bad decisions and incentives built around traditional costing ideas belie this argument. If systems aren't being used, why is there so much *mis*use?

"Throughput, Not Cost, Determines Profitability."   Some authorities claim that emphasizing a seemingly less-profitable product actually brings more to the bottom line because it is better suited to maximizing utilization within operational constraints. An ABM system, however, in its separate reporting of downtime and idle capacity costs with causes, would alert management to the real situation. For example, the identification of causes through ABM reporting would indicate that "machine X was down today because we were running product B, which does not utilize that resource."

"The Benefits of Accuracy Do Not Justify Its Cost."   Because of inherent, random differences between models and the real world, an ABM system can never attain 100 percent accuracy. But even a simple ABM system comes much closer than a traditional costing system. The ultimate arbiter of system complexity is cost-benefit analysis. If the system is 95 percent accurate, is it worth spending an additional $100,000 to make it 96 percent accurate?

Another aspect of the compromise deals with the "conventional" approach to ABM. Designers were encouraged to use as activity drivers data that were already being captured by the system. Compromises to model quality became commonplace. Data on activity drivers requiring less effort to accumulate were substituted for others that better reflected causal relationships. The use of the new approach to ABM suggested in this book removes these concerns because it eliminates the need to collect activity-driver data.

"ABM Doesn't Apply to Service Businesses."   An unfortunate attitude of service business managers, brought up with traditional accounting ideas, seems to say that costing can be done only in manufacturing. The numerous examples related to service companies provided in Chapter 4 and throughout this text refute that belief. Costs affect not only pricing of services but their very design and definition.

Lack of New Information

Hard as it is to believe, some still argue that ABM offers no new information for decision making.

"ABM Is Nothing New."   A glance at any cost accounting textbook should be sufficient to quell this statement. ABM represents a change in the underlying idea of cost accounting that is truly innovative. It encompasses the best of the cost systems designed in the past, but in a way that is universally applicable.

"Results of ABM Won't Affect Selling Prices."   If the market determines selling price, ABM takes on another important role: that of assessing profitability of the various products and customers involved. It may uncover a profitable niche that has been overlooked, or lead to deemphasis of a certain product line.

"We Already Have Standards for Costing Output."   While standards stated in units that may be used as activity drivers are useful in implementing ABM, the costs attached to them are not. Traditional standard costing aggregates and averages costs over units, whereas ABM traces costs to what's actually caused by the activity.

Radical Nature

When it is finally admitted that ABM represents a substantial change, new arguments emerge.

"Why Now, All of a Sudden?"   Managers who have done without an adequate information system for so long may question why they need one now. As demonstrated in subsequent chapters, ABM can affect the outcome of nearly every significant business decision. Today, the technology is available to a degree that managers can obtain the advantages of information for decisions at reasonable cost.

"Too Many New Answers"   The biggest barrier with respect to the information ABM provides is the overwhelming number of issues it may bring to light. How should management react to unprofitable products? The answer lies either in the activity drivers or in pricing. Activity drivers provide the causes of costs. You can cut costs by reducing either the quantity of drivers per product or the cost per unit of a driver. You may also adjust pricing to reflect whatever special services the customers are getting that are causing the losses to occur. For example, a customization charge may be appropriate.

Easing the Transition

Compromises exist between full-scale implementation and a more gradual approach. For example:

1. Designating of an area of the company for a pilot project
2. Utilizing a stand-alone module, say for estimating and strategic decisions, without integrating the underlying accounting system

These two options provide acceptable ways of easing the transition. Being relegated to a "second system," however, may detract from ABM's power and reduce priority for its maintenance. Over the long term, a goal of full integration is preferred.

As is implicit in these comments, the reporting, goal setting, costing, and other ABM functions are overwhelming if taken in a single dose. While from a control standpoint a flexible budget is the top priority, marketing's desire for better cost estimates often wins out. This can easily lead back to a control priority.

EASING IMPLEMENTATION

The highest priority for ABM is often the generation of detailed costs for use in estimating. Once the format has been generalized, sales and estimating people must be trained in its use. This may raise doubts. "How can the high-volume product actually cost so little? We would be operating at a loss if we priced based on that cost." Or, "We'll never get away with charging that much for a low-volume product!" The challenge becomes whether costs will truly be fully absorbed by the new system. At this point, flexible budgeting enters the picture; nothing proves the accuracy of a model as much as the monthly monitoring of results. Suddenly, ABM becomes the means for controlling costs.

Finally, ABM becomes part of the strategic decision-making process. ABM ideas are used in business planning, marketing strategy, operational decisions, and so on. We'll see how in upcoming chapters.

Summary

Understanding how ABM applies to your operation is essential to leading an effective implementation. Constructing the resource usage path is an essential first step. The next chapter is devoted entirely to presenting ABM systems in diverse industries.

4

Monitoring Key Data with ABM Cost-Cause Grids and Resource Usage Paths

Not only are resource usage paths convenient summaries of ABM system; they are useful analytical tools from which to derive cost-cause grids. The initial effort of constructing a resource usage path is worthwhile because it has so many immediate applications. For example, activity drivers can easily be used as key statistics for improving operations, helping the organization focus its attention on meeting certain goals. Perhaps only a few goals are in effect at any given time, but once they are reached, new goals take effect to suit the next most important need for improvement. In this way, activity drivers support continuous improvement in operations.

Activity drivers and other statistics are so important to the benefits of ABM that a sample listing is provided in Compendium I. This list is intended to stimulate your thinking not only as to what your company's potential activity drivers might be but also as to its key statistics.

This chapter offers in-depth examples of ABM systems in diverse business settings. They will help you to become comfortable with the idea of modeling cost-flow ("resource usage") patterns. In each example, we trace the causes of costs through to product output, without their being affected by other unidentified drivers. Irrelevant costs are cleared away.

Now we'll put the resource usage path to work in the following diverse industries.

- Bank
- Delivery service
- General contractor
- Hospital
- Local government
- Accounting firm
- Steel service company

- Machine shop
- Metal foundry

Each example begins with a case study that introduces the issues to be addressed. The study is followed by an analysis of the company's activities, together with an ABM resource usage path.

Bank

BANK CORP.

Bank Corp.'s loan portfolio is growing rapidly. It needs to balance additional resources for loan servicing against outsourcing alternatives. In order to determine which areas are worth continuing, it must have cost information on a per-service transaction basis.

Results: ABM provides data not only for determining staffing needs but also for comparing its existing operations to outsourcing alternatives and industry benchmarks. The bank decides to farm out its loss leaders and retain sources of its competitive advantages.

The traditional bank's major asset is its investments, a majority of which are in loan portfolios. Its largest liability and source of funds is from the cash of depositors. Interest revenue generated from the loans is used to pay interest to depositors, investment costs, and depositor service costs.

Faced with increasing competition, the variety of service options, and automation, the banking industry is ripe for ABM. With the growth in specialized businesses to which servicing may be assigned or outsourced, it is essential to cost each service on an a la carte basis. Bundled services are no longer the sole alternative.

The resource usage path in Exhibit 4-1 shows the support and operating activities necessary in a bank.

Direct Activities

For illustrative purposes, the direct activities associated with depositor services, "direct: services," are distinguished from investments, "direct: investments." The support activities are fairly typical.[1]

---

[1] Proofing is the function through which direct activities are routed for verification.

Exhibit 4-1. Resource Usage Path: Bank

Level I Drivers	Support Activities	Level II Drivers	Operating Activities	Costs
• Related transactions • Square footage • Head count • Transaction volume • Files, transactions • Direct charge • Value, remaining life • Head count, payroll dollars	**Support** Administrative Occupancy Personnel services Quality control Computer services Depreciation Payroll fringe	• Discretionary	**Discretionary** Capacity decisions Training Cost of capital	**Resource Usage** Services provided
		• Checks paid, stop payments processed, checks returned • Deposits processed • Statements, accounts • Checks certified, cashiers' checks	**Direct: Services** Checking services Deposit activities Reporting Other services	
		• Applications, loans, appraisals • Loans, delinquencies, transactions, payoffs • Transactions	**Direct: Investments** Load origination Load servicing Other investing	
		• Specific customers, borrowers	**Special Requirements** Special services	

Although labor-intensive, the direct activities can be standardized. As long as a comparison of actual and estimated costs is shown in the budget, there is no need for a time-reporting system. But time reporting, at least on a temporary basis, may help in refining the model.

Direct Activities: Services Because the case study addresses investment activities, services will not be covered in detail other than to say that they include those relating to depositors. Service activities somewhat resemble those of a batch or repetitive manufacturer, and may be driven by such processes as number of checks paid, stop payments processed, checks certified, checks returned, and statements issued.

Direct Activities: Investments Consistent with the focus of the case study, loan servicing costs are chosen for analysis. Investment activities include loan origination, loan servicing, and other investing and are detailed in Exhibit 4-2, the cost-cause grid.

Applying servicing costs on number of loans alone oversimplifies cost incurrence. Real estate tax compliance, for example, more properly relates to the number of tax identification numbers, which may vary. The following summarizes the related direct activities:

- *Transaction processing.* These activities include routine loan accounting and transaction processing performed by bookkeeping personnel. Specifically, the activities encompass processing of cash receipts, cash disbursements, monthly closings, monthly statements, loan payoffs, annual IRS reporting, and loan confirmations. Number of transactions and loans are appropriate costing bases.

- *Reporting.* Routine reports include notifications regarding borrower compliance, accounting reports, monthly remittances, and financial statement analyses, which can be applied on a per report basis or over the number of loans, as appropriate.

Certain loan categories may require highly specialized reporting, which can be covered under special requirements activities.

- *Insurance review.* These activities encompass compliance review of insurance documents, correspondence, and filing. Efficiencies can be obtained by combining building, rents, and liability policies, making policy review an activity that is partly lot-driven. Insurance policies and loans cover most other costs.

- *Analysis.* Financial statement review, correspondence, and filing are a bank's main analysis activities. Certain noncompliance risks also exist,

Exhibit 4-2. Loan Servicing Cost-Cause Grid: Bank

Level II Drivers ("Cause")	*Operating Activities* ("Cost")
	Direct: Loan Servicing
♦ Transactions	Transaction processing
♦ Reports, complexity	Reporting
♦ Insurance policies	Insurance review
♦ Analyses, statements	Analysis
♦ Inspections	Inspection
♦ Properties	Tax compliance
♦ Escrow accounts	Escrow maintenance
♦ Delinquent loans	Delinquency servicing

including noncomplying formats, missing information, defaults, and extensions. Drivers include financial statements and loans. This category may also include lease review and correspondence, driven by lessors, significant leases, and tenants.

♦ *Property inspection.* Activities include performing, reporting, and reviewing inspections. Number of inspections and distance are activity drivers.

♦ *Real estate tax compliance.* The activities include the various correspondence, phone calls, and record keeping associated with payment verification. Properties, property identification numbers, and loans are bases for assigning costs. As with insurance, costs of following up on noncomplying borrowers can be significant.

♦ *Escrow maintenance.* Escrow accounts may be maintained for certain loans. The costs may be assigned over the number of escrow accounts, properties, or loans to which they apply.

♦ *Delinquency and bad-debt risks.* Although related to delinquencies rather than routine servicing, management may prefer that average costs be reflected in estimating on a per-loan basis. Included in the activity are the loss of principal and interest, delinquent notices, collection efforts, and legal involvement. Because a small number of problem borrowers create the costs, it is considered optional whether these costs should be applied at the servicing level. Ideally, the risk factor would vary according to a risk classification defined for the various classifications of loans within the portfolio.

Discretionary Activities

Activities listed as discretionary include:

- *Capacity decisions.* While they may also relate to facilities, most capacity decisions concern personnel. Overtime or excess staffing create costs that are not attributable to service costing. Rather, the costs result from management decisions, and should be segregated as such.
- *Training.* In part a result of management policies, training is another major discretionary category. Balancing the efficiencies of new hires against overtime through ABM is among the topics of the next chapter.
- *Cost of capital.* This cost is discretionary because it does not affect the costs of services provided, although it definitely has a substantial impact on profitability.

Special Requirements Activities

Special requirements include those costs not covered in the direct or discretionary categories. They could include, for example, loan servicing noncompliance costs that would be directly charged.

As a servicing function grows, efficiencies may be attained by creating so-called skilled positions for specialized tasks and relegating clerical functions to appropriate levels. Other areas for improved efficiency indicated by ABM may include automation of correspondence, use of centralized reminder files for items such as tax payment due dates, and systems for loan file tracking. Improving efficiency is the subject of Chapter 5.

As mentioned in the case study, management looked to the ABM budget for answers about how and whether to expand services. A comprehensive look at the ABM costs per activity driver is given in Exhibit 4-3 for the bank's loan servicing function. Armed with these costs, management can link budgeted operating expenses directly to consumption of cost-driver quantities by the activity. Finally, decisions relating to outsourcing and service profitability are based on sound information.

Delivery Service

DELIVERY SERVICE LTD.

Delivery Service Ltd. found its market becoming more and more competitive. It was aware of the average cost per stop on a route, but not of how much these

Exhibit 4-3. ABM Cost per Activity Driver: Bank Loan Servicing Co.

COMMERCIAL MORTGAGE DIVISION BUDGET

Activity, Activity Driver	Annual Rate
Delinquency risk, per loan	$ 73.76
Financial analysis, per statement	113.35
Insurance escrow maintenance, per account	35.47
Insurance review, per insurance policy	65.75
Investor remittance, per remit	51.50
Investor reporting, per loan	24.25
Loan accounting, per loan	97.20
Property inspection, per inspection	110.98
Tax escrow maintenance, per property	27.82
Tax payment verification, per tax bill	17.44

Key data for ABM are costs per unit of driver. For example, if applied to actual quantities of cost driver incurred in a given period, a predictive budget can be generated.

costs could vary. Essential variables in profit were not reflected in its analysis. The company turns to ABM.

Results: When ABM is applied, transit time and route costs are finally recognized and quantified in cost terms. With this information, the company is able to become more competitive in certain markets, and deemphasize others. The result is a more profitable business, focused on the most advantageous markets. In the process, management has gained a tool for understanding and controlling costs.

Delivery services can include various operations subject to route costing. The discussion that follows applies to many types of delivery service operations.

Several characteristics of the example operation are notable:

1. Delivery vehicles are taken from headquarters each morning for their assigned routes. The distance to and density of any particular route may vary.

2. In relation to time spent at stops, time in transit per route may vary from a ratio 1:1 to 3:1. This means that transit time is at least as significant or up to three times as significant as time at stops.

3. Normally, after pickup, the load is retained at the storage facility overnight. Drop-off is scheduled for the next day on the most convenient route.

4. Certain customers require same-day pickup and delivery, meaning that both pickup and drop-off must occur within a single route.

The company bases its costing on the following:

- Labor time per stop, estimated according to guidelines that cover average stop and in-transit time
- Labor time per stop multiplied by average pay, to which is added overhead as a percentage of labor

With this understanding of the operation, the following conclusions can be reached:

- Major determinants of cost include transit time, miles, routes, and stop density. Present costing doesn't consider them.
- Route costs include time in transit, mileage from headquarters, vehicle depreciation, insurance, and other costs associated with routes. While these costs are fixed when considering an additional stop for any particular route, the routes themselves are variable, in that unprofitable ones may be discontinued.
- Inefficiencies such as overtime, downtime, and training are averaged in to overhead rates, overburdening estimates with costs that the new order may not cause.
- The cost of same-day service is not determinable under the present costing method.

A resource usage path for Delivery Service Ltd. is presented in Exhibit 4-4. It separates direct pickup and delivery activities from transit associated with the route, "route activities."

Support Activities

The categories of support activities include supervision, occupancy, personnel, dispatch, vehicle maintenance, insurance, depreciation, payroll fringe, and other administrative functions.

Exhibit 4-4. Resource Usage Path: Delivery Service

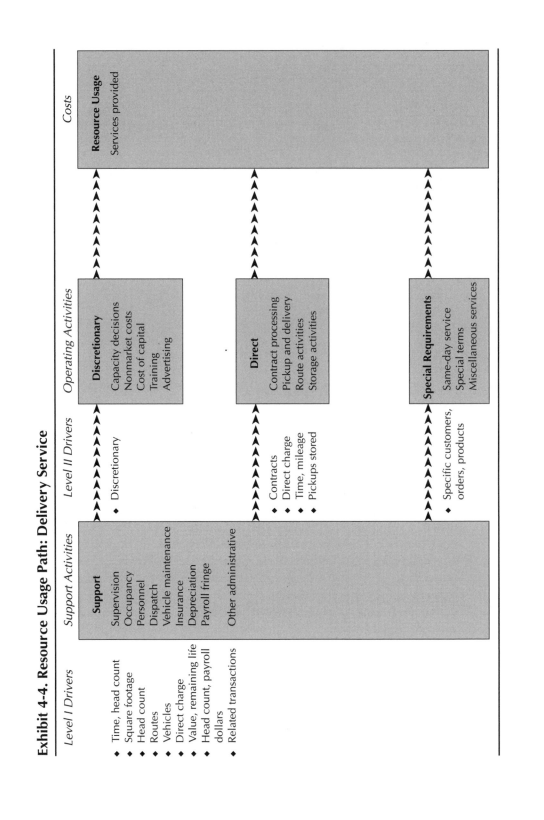

Level I Drivers	Support Activities	Level II Drivers	Operating Activities		Costs

Support Activities

Support

Supervision
Occupancy
Personnel
Dispatch
Vehicle maintenance
Insurance
Depreciation
Payroll fringe

Other administrative

Level I Drivers

- Time, head count
- Square footage
- Head count
- Routes
- Vehicles
- Direct charge
- Value, remaining life
- Head count, payroll dollars
- Related transactions

Level II Drivers

- Discretionary

- Contracts
- Direct charge
- Time, mileage
- Pickups stored

- Specific customers, orders, products

Operating Activities

Discretionary

Capacity decisions
Nonmarket costs
Cost of capital
Training
Advertising

Direct

Contract processing
Pickup and delivery
Route activities
Storage activities

Special Requirements

Same-day service
Special terms
Miscellaneous services

Costs

Resource Usage

Services provided

Discretionary Activities

Discretionary activities for the delivery service are fairly typical.

Direct Activities

Direct activities are as follows:

- *Contract processing.* Costs of processing, billing, and accounting for contracts are included in this category. The costs are driven by the number of contracts, since substantially all are billed monthly.
- *Pickup and delivery.* The costs of these activities are driven by time at the stop and mileage. This category covers all direct, incremental costs attributable to an additional stop. Note that mileage from the point of pickup to delivery may either be added to reflect costs of same-day service requests or be classified as special requirements.
- *Route activities.* In the context of accepting an additional stop on a route, route-activity costs are considered fixed; however, any route is variable. Payroll and related costs of time in transit are driven by time. Variable vehicle and related costs for round-trip mileage from headquarters use number of miles as the activity driver, whereas fixed costs such as depreciation and licensing use number of routes. Number of routes also drives insurance and certain other overhead costs. Where determinable, additional insurance costs from risks associated with particular routes should be directly charged.
- *Storage activities.* Storage costs are incurred for those pickups routinely stored overnight. Costs are assigned on the basis of number of pickups stored.

Special Requirements

As in other contexts, special requirements represent those activities not reflected as direct or discretionary. For example, certain customers may need the items picked up to be verified or packaged. If infrequent, these may fall under a "special services" category; if substantial, they would justify analysis in the form of a detailed direct activity costing.

Depending on the information systems already available for scheduling and billing, budgeting of activity drivers may be entirely automated. Data elements from contracts necessary for implementation include:

- Pickup and delivery activity drivers
  - —Time spent at stop
  - —Incremental mileage
- Route activity drivers
  - —Number of routes
  - —Transit time, which may be derived from total time less time at stops
  - —Mileage to and from headquarters
- Other activity drivers
  - —For contract processing: the number of contracts
  - —For the storage facility: loads held overnight, which could be derived from total pickups less those subject to same-day service

As Delivery Service Ltd.'s management may have already discovered, the traditional costing model shown in Exhibit 4-5 fails to adequately reflect the company's underlying operations. Time spent at stops is applied a costing rate intended to reflect labor and overhead. The rate does not consider variations between routes arising from transit time, mileage, and stop density, nor does it show the need to recover fixed route costs. Each stop carries an equal cost per minute, which is not correct.

Exhibit 4-5. Traditional Costing Approach: Delivery Service

Description	Rate	Usage	Route A Extension	Route B Extension
Stops, route A	$1.50/min.	120	$180	
Stops, route B		240		$360
Total cost			$180	$360
Stops			20	40
Cost per stop			9	9
Revenue per stop			$ 12	$ 12
Net profit (loss) per stop				$ 3

The traditional method used here is akin to a job cost, where costs are based on chargeable direct labor time. Time spent at stops is considered chargeable. The method ignores the significant other costs involved in the service. As Exhibit 4-6 demonstrates, the oversimplicity of this method distorts profit-and-loss implications.

Exhibit 4-6. ABM Costing Approach: Delivery Service

Description	Rate	Usage	Route A Extension	Route B Extension
Route costs:				
In-transit	$.30/min.	360 (A)	$108	
		140 (B)		$ 72
	$.20/mi.	100 (A)	20	
		50 (B)		10
Other route costs	$75/route	1	75	75
Subtotal, route costs			$203	$157
Direct costs:				
Stops	$.30/min.	120 (A)	$ 36	
		240 (B)		$ 72
	$.20/mi.	50 (A)	10	
		50 (B)		10
Contract processing	$1/order	20 (A)	20	
		40 (B)		40
Special requirements			0	0
Subtotal, direct costs			$ 66	$122
TOTAL			$269	$279
Stops			20	40
Cost per stop			$ 13.5	$ 7
Revenue per stop			$ 12.0	$ 12
Net profit (loss) per stop			($ 1.5)	$ 5
Net profit (loss) per route			($ 29)	$201

For the delivery service, conventional costing fails to provide true profitability information. While the service may not necessarily discontinue route A in the near term, through ABM it can set a target for breakeven purposes.

In contrast, the ABM approach shown in Exhibit 4-6 considers the significant aspects of route profitability. According to the ABM costing form shown in the exhibit, a route with a high number of stops now becomes measurably more profitable than one with fewer. With this information, it becomes possible to develop a breakeven point that must be attained if a route is to become profitable.

The cost-estimating form could also function on a stop level. That alternative, shown in Exhibit 4-7, entails the assignment of route costs to

Exhibit 4-7. Assignment of Route Costs to Orders: Delivery Service

Assumptions

Stop A:	3 min.
Stop B:	15 min.
Total time at stops:	180 min.
Total stops on route:	40
Total time in transit:	5 hr.
Total route costs to be allocated:	$360

Allocations

Per stop
Route cost per stop ($360/40)	$ 9
Cost allocated to stop A	9
Cost allocated to stop B	9

Per minute at stop
Route cost per minute at stop ($360/180)	$ 2
Cost allocated to stop A	6
Cost allocated to stop B	30

Because route costs are fixed when additional stops are being considered, the selection of allocation method is a policy decision for which more than one approach is acceptable. The allocations illustrated include a per-stop basis and a time-at-stop basis. The first tends to penalize short stops, whereas the second assumes that route costs vary with direct time.

stops. Relative to an incremental stop, route costs are fixed. How to assign these costs for detailed costing is up to the user. There is no single correct answer.

Note that if route costs are assigned on a per-stop basis, the smaller stops suffer. If, on the other hand, they are assigned according to time at the stop, costs follow chargeable time, which may also be the basis for billing. Obviously, management should adopt the format that is most useful.

General Contractor

GENERAL CONTRACTOR CO.

General Contractor Co. cannot bid accurately on projects or predict profits and losses. Its traditional labor-based method for applying overhead appears adequate for the carpentry portion of its business, but carpentry is only a small portion of the company's total costs. The remaining costs seem difficult to monitor or control. General Contractor Co. applies ABM to get a better handle on costs.

Results: While its initial objective is to improve the bidding function, uses quickly spread to controlling costs and operations.

The construction industry is extremely diverse, encompassing construction of buildings, streets, tunnels, and so on. From a cost-system standpoint, issues of concern include bidding, project management, subcontracting, and joint venturing.

From this diverse industry, general building contractors have been selected for illustration. The general building contractor's function is less related to direct labor than it is to project management and oversight of subcontractors, so overhead costs are relatively significant. Activities performed are recapped in the resource usage path shown in Exhibit 4-8. Clearly, only a small portion of the costs of these diverse activities can be related to direct labor or sales volume.

Support Activities

Support activities include the following:

◆ *Corporate office management and administration.* The traditional system of costing does not reflect the variation of general and administrative costs with levels of activity. ABM recognizes that certain of these costs apply equally by the project, not withstanding the project's size. For example, credit approval, order processing, job-cost record maintenance, billing, accounts receivable maintenance, or collection may vary with the number of projects, invoices, and customers. Costs may be associated with certain types of contracts. For example, the need to provide the owner with cost documentation in "cost-plus" arrangements may represent a significant administrative cost that managers should consider when bidding that type of work. As to fixed costs, if you tried to recover a month's office expense and officer's salary with each bid, few bids, if any, would be accepted. The key is to spread these costs over a "normal" volume base. If certain customers demand more than their fair share of attention by the corporate office, those costs should be reflected in future bids.

◆ *Procurement costs.* Once the owner has accepted the bid, the process of releasing purchase orders and seriously considering contractors for outsourced work begins. Purchasing costs tend to vary according to the number of orders released and the number of vendors involved. Contrac-

Exhibit 4-8. Resource Usage Path: General Contractor

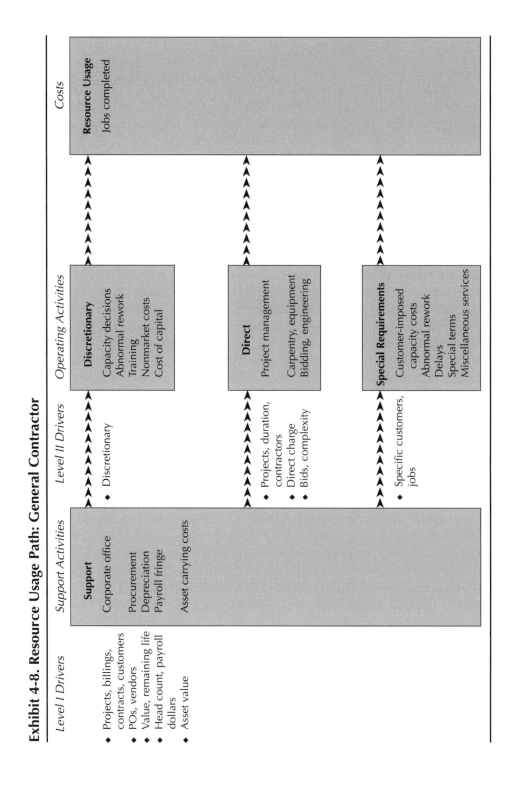

tors routinely dealt with may carry lower procurement cost than new ones. As with vendors, the lowest-priced contractor does not necessarily equal the lowest cost. Untried contractors must be thoroughly considered; a wrong decision can result in late or shoddy performance, causing delay and disorganization at the job site, not to mention the owner's bad will.

◆ *Asset-carrying costs.* A complex array of variables may be identified as "driving" carrying costs relating to materials and equipment. While the price advantages of volume buying and entering blanket contracts are clear, they are offset by the cost of carrying inventory; this includes financing, warehousing, insurance, and shrinkage. Overhead relating to equipment includes depreciation, repairs, maintenance, fuel, certain indirect labor, and financing. Ideally, these costs are accumulated in a separate cost center, similar to a job profit center, and charged to jobs at hourly rates so that projects of long duration bear their fair share of the costs. Fixed costs such as depreciation that do not vary with levels of activity should be charged according to expected normal operating hours, not history. Otherwise, you run the risk of overpricing equipment, which leads to lower usage, which in turn leads to higher pricing and even less usage. As for variable costs, certain ones, such as fuel and repairs, may vary according to the intensity of usage rather than time at the job site. Selection of the appropriate "activity drivers" is essential in assessing true profits.

◆ *Other support activities.* Other support activities include depreciation and payroll fringe, which have been covered elsewhere.

Discretionary Activities

Discretionary activities touch on familiar areas. Because of the use of contractors and trade union labor, excess capacity is less likely to occur for general contractors. Likewise, overtime and downtime tend to be chargeable to jobs.

Direct Activities

Direct activities include the following:

◆ *Project management.* These activities tend to vary with the number and complexity of jobs in process, the number and variety of contractors engaged, special or unique requirements of the owner, and project scope and duration. Some may be incurred in fulfilling responsibility for General's part of the job. General site overhead such as rent and security may vary most directly with time or duration of the project.

Many contingencies also exist, as follows:
   —Weather conditions
   —Cost escalation, e.g., from inflation, union negotiations
   —Adverse site conditions
   —Late design specifications
   —Responsibility disputes between crafts

Management should consult history for additional costs and their likelihood under a given set of circumstances.

   ◆ *Project performance, including carpentry and equipment.* The direct costs incurred by the general contractor in performing its portion of the work is the one activity that traditional systems purport to cover. But even in this area, traditional costing deals with such costs as indirect labor, supervision, equipment costs, and job-site overhead summarily in one factor. Similarly, rework, excessive moving or material handling, idle time, overtime, supplier overage, and scrap costs may be inadequately tracked, causing those inefficiencies to be factored in to all future estimates—regardless of whether those events are likely to occur—creating the potential for noncompetitive bids. The nature of these costs and the causes of their incurrence are lost. In addition, costing should consider the chargeability of highly specialized trades, particularly where salaries, licensing, and costs of ongoing training are significant. Assuming, as in many systems, that only salary and fringe represent job "cost" is misleading.

   ◆ *Bidding and engineering.* Far from relating to direct labor or sales, bidding costs depend on the number of projects bid, their complexity, and many other factors unique to projects. You would naturally avoid bidding on:
   —An overseas project for which travel costs alone would do away
      with potential margin
   —Nonroutine small projects that fail to carry sufficient margin

   Ideally, to ease the decision of when to bid, these intuitive reactions would have a quantitative basis.

Special Requirements

Treatment of special requirements is similar to that described for other industries. Chargeable costs should be reflected in assessing order and customer profitability, whereas nonchargeable or discretionary ones indicative of inefficiency call for separate reporting with causes, to ensure visibility.

The cost-estimating form developed by management will be presented in Chapter 8.

Hospital

HOSPITAL, INC.

Hospital, Inc.'s cost system is considered sophisticated by industry standards, but it is not sophisticated enough to provide the details needed to support decisions. Special services, for example, cannot be adequately costed, nor can make-or-buy analyses be supported. Management applies ABM.

Results: ABM provides a level of detail that satisfies management's needs. Needs for special services and insourcing are fulfilled as well.

With concerns about the rise in costs of health care, analyzing hospital costs is not new. ABM, however, can dramatically improve on traditional analysis.

Methods used for hospitals suffer from the following deficiencies:

◆ Support and nonrevenue-producing cost centers may be charged directly and entirely against revenue centers, without cost-cause justification.
◆ Most costs are treated as indirect activities, even though analysis indicates that they might be better classified as direct.
◆ Cost allocations amount to averaging techniques that are not well suited to detailed service costing.

Given these characteristics, these methods offer little insight into controlling costs or acquiring service-cost knowledge.

At conflict with overly simplified techniques is the need to distinguish special and routine services for insurance reimbursement purposes. As demonstrated in previous examples, ABM is designed to capture and distinguish special requirements. In addition, by tracing through major activities, it becomes possible to assign costs accurately without making arbitrary allocations.

The resource usage path for Hospital, Inc., is shown in Exhibit 4-9.

Support Activities

With the exception of pharmacy and cafeteria, the supporting activities listed have appeared in other models. For pharmacy activities, issues of

Exhibit 4-9. Resource Usage Path: Hospital

Level I Drivers	Support Activities	Level II Drivers	Operating Activities	Costs
	Support		**Discretionary**	**Resource Usage**
♦ Related transactions	Administrative	♦ Discretionary	Capacity decisions	Services provided
♦ Square footage	Occupancy		Training	
♦ Head count	Personnel services		Cost of capital	
♦ Issues	Pharmacy		Community services	
♦ Food value	Cafeteria			
♦ Tests, complexity	Laboratory		**Direct**	
♦ Value, remaining life	Depreciation	♦ Patients	Admission, records, billing activities	
♦ Head count, payroll dollars	Payroll fringe	♦ Direct charge	Food, medicine, chargeable services	
		♦ Contacts	Routine nursing	
		♦ Patient days	Patient room	
			Special Requirements	
		♦ Specific patients	Outside consultations	
			Special services	

stock are an appropriate activity driver; for cafeteria activities, the relative food value may be used in lieu of a more detailed cost-control system.

Discretionary and Special Requirements Activities

Discretionary and special requirements activities present no special problems. As with a hotel, capacity utilization may be measured in terms of rooms. For billing, special services reporting may be highly significant.

Direct Activities

Finally, direct activities may be analyzed as follows:

- ◆ *Admission, records, and billing.* These activities share a common element in that they vary according to the number of patients, although records may document the complexity.
- ◆ *Food, medicine, and chargeable services.* Where costs are directly traced to patients, direct charge is most desirable. If the pharmacy and equipment storage areas maintain perpetual inventory records and the cafeteria bills sales, direct charges should create no special problems.
- ◆ *Routine nursing.* Nursing and other activities routinely performed may best be allocated rather than directly charged. Number of contacts is an appropriate base for nursing.
- ◆ *Patient rooms.* Outside of real estate, hospitals are the rare instance where occupancy activities may be classified as direct. Number of patient days on a "normalized" basis is an appropriate driver.

Equipped with this information, management can face decision making with new confidence. It can predict the effects of alternatives that previously it could only guess at.

Local Government

LOCAL GOVERNMENT

Under increasing political pressure to control costs, Local Government has been forced to consider efficiency and reexamine the need for certain services. ABM can provide an essential tool for this purpose.

Today, even government needs to understand the costs of its services. Where government competes with the private sector, ABM provides the basis for comparing costs. ABM can also help to determine fees for services, where applicable. State and local regulations may even require cost analysis, when government must limit user charges to the cost of the services.

While government is not unfamiliar with the idea of cost consciousness, it will still find ABM to be a radical departure from traditional methods. The cost methodology under the federal Medicare system, for example, tends to oversimplify operations. Disregarding actual causes, it routinely allocates administrative overhead as a percentage of directly charged costs.

The costing problems found most commonly in government include:

- Intertwining of various divisions and departments, which may be providing hidden subsidies such as payroll fringe and facilities
- Use of expenditure accounting that does not relate asset cost to the periods benefited
- Averaging, perpetuated by regulatory reporting formats

Exhibit 4-10 shows the resource usage path for Local Government's inspection division. From an external perspective, its services, and their costs, are extremely diverse. Citizens with a rodent problem may be charged for inspection services. Restaurant owners may be required to undergo inspection as part of licensing, which carries a set fee. Finally, environmental hazard inspections may precede condemnation of property, without collection of a fee.

Many of the activities and drivers are similar to those of for-profit businesses. The support, discretionary, and special requirements activities for Local Government offer little that is new.

Direct Activities

The direct activities are as follows:

- *Licenses.* Once an organization has passed inspection, the processing of licenses is fairly routine and may be assigned over the quantity of applications.
- *Inspection fieldwork.* Direct charge, although requiring time reporting, benefits not only costing but assessment of efficiency and staffing.
- *Travel, vehicle.* As with the delivery service, these costs need to be analyzed separately from provision of the services. Route and other efficiencies may become apparent.

Exhibit 4-10. Resource Usage Path: Government Health Inspection

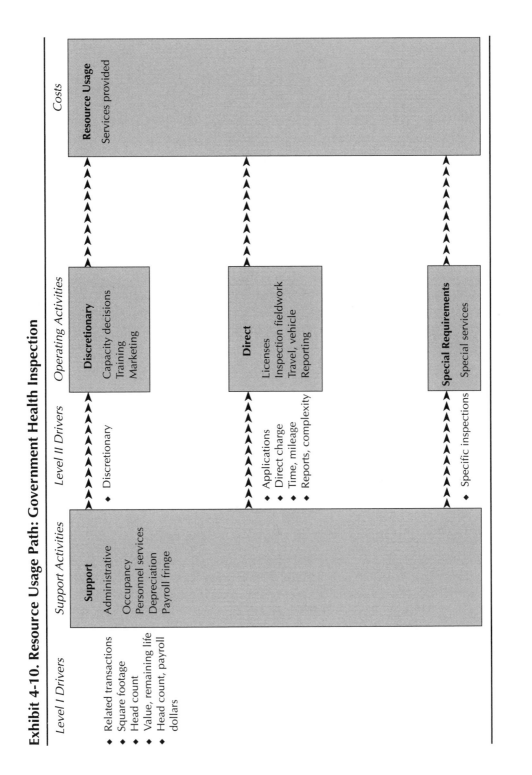

♦ *Reporting.* Reports generated and their relative complexity determine reporting activity costs.

What is picked up in the analysis is that certain expenditures, such
as those for identifying environmental hazards, are strictly for public
safety. Other expenditures, such as for licensing, may vary significantly in
cost but are provided for a set fee. And still others, such as rodent control,
may be performed by the private sector. The analysis may lead to the
following decisions:

♦ Restaurants requiring multiple inspections should be charged for
those inspections.
♦ Rodent control may be performed more competitively by the private sector, and related government programs should be discontinued.

Undoubtedly, ABM has the potential to revolutionize the governmental
sector as much as it has other industries.

Accounting Firm

ACCOUNTING FIRM

Accounting Firm has invested in new, innovative service areas, but its cost
reporting system does not allow for determining their profitability. It tries ABM.

Results: The information becomes available on a routine basis.

The resource usage path for Accounting Firm is illustrated in Exhibit
4-11. While an accounting firm was chosen for illustration, it should be
pointed out that other professional firms tend to exhibit the same pattern.
Because of the significance of payroll as a cost as well as a billing activity,
professional firms are likely to have time-reporting systems in place, akin
to a manufacturing job cost. Support activities include continuing education, assigned to activities based on direct charge of time and costs.
Discretionary activities include practice development, another name for
marketing and client retention activities. Special requirements are similar
to those discussed elsewhere.

Exhibit 4-11. Resource Usage Path: Accounting Firm

Level I Drivers	Support Activities	Level II Drivers	Operating Activities	Costs
◆ Related transactions ◆ Head count, payroll dollars ◆ Square footage ◆ Direct charge	**Support** Administrative Payroll fringe Occupancy Continuing education	◆ Discretionary	**Discretionary** Capacity decisions Practice development Cost of capital Nonmarket costs	**Resource Usage** Services provided
		◆ Direct charge ◆ Processing time ◆ Customers ◆ Services	**Direct** Professional services Computer processing Customer activities Service development	
		◆ Specific customers, projects	**Special Requirements** Customer-imposed capacity costs Special services	

Direct Activities

Direct activities are as follows:

- *Professional services.* With payroll being the largest cost, time reporting is used for direct charges of costs to projects. Downtime and other
nonchargeable time can easily be charged to the appropriate support or
discretionary activity category.

- *Computer processing.* Computer processing may justify an exception
to traditional labor time reporting. Accounting firms may perform general
ledger, payroll, accounts receivable, or other functions for their clients.
The firm may have made a substantial investment in computer hardware
and software that it wishes to recover. Apart from labor time, jobs may be
queued for overnight or daily processing while other jobs are being keyed
in. Certain reporting formats, organizations, and other aspects may cause
substantial variation in the time it takes the computer to run a particular
job. These aspects are not accounted for in the traditional approach to
costing, illustrated in Exhibit 4-12. Compare this to the ABM approach in
Exhibit 4-13. Run time is costed separately from input time, using separate
billing rates. If the variables associated with differing jobs are quantified
in the form of drivers, however, those could be substituted for the tracking
of actual time if tested through the budgeting process, e.g., number of
report pages.

- *Customer activities.* Costs that are not service-related could be assigned to this category.

- *Service development.* This category is the answer to management's
need for investments in new service areas. Under ABM, these costs are
segregated for management's scrutiny.

Steel Service Company

STEEL SERVICE COMPANY

Steel Service Company is a slitting operation that generates a substantial
amount of off-fall material. Off-fall costing includes the full value of metal and
processing. Costing in this manner, management has come to realize that its
inventory is full of hidden losses. As the off-fall was scrapped, the losses began
to materialize. Management concludes that orders generating the off-fall should
have taken the hit all along. It decides to try ABM.

Exhibit 4-12. Traditional Approach: Accounting Firm

COMPUTER SERVICE CHARGE

Description	Billing Rate	Usage	Service A Extension	Service B Extension
Data entry and review	$2/min.	20 min. (A)	$40	
		20 min. (B)		$40
Total billing			$40	$40

Accounting firms may bill computer services on the basis of direct labor time, even though other aspects of the service may be as significant. Exhibit 4-13 offers an alternative approach.

Exhibit 4-13. ABM Approach: Accounting Firm

COMPUTER SERVICE CHARGE

Description	Billing Rate	Usage	Service A Extension	Service B Extension
Data entry and review	$1/min.	20 min. (A)	$20	
		20 min. (B)		$20
Computer processing	$1/min.	10 min. (A)	10	
		30 min. (B)		30
Total billing			$30	$50

The ABM approach recognizes the separate nature of entry and processing services performed for customers. Where jobs are too unique to be standardized, a time base may be appropriate for ABM. Note that if work could be measured on the basis of its characteristics, time bases would no longer be necessary.

Results: For the first time, management begins to see a true picture of order profitability. Assignment of an appropriate scrap value to off-fall as it is generated results in proper costing of orders filled, since the losses are charged to the orders currently.

Steel service companies slit and package steel coils. The slitting operation takes coiled metal approximately 36 inches wide and several thousand feet long (called master coils) and cuts them lengthwise to provide narrower coils to customer specifications. The work area layout is designed to receive master coils at one end of the plant, slit the coils to order in the middle, and ship finished coils at the other end.

Several aspects of our sample operation are notable:

- The machines use a "loop" slitting technique to ensure highly accurate widths of coils produced. Machine speeds are in feet per minute, with some variance depending on gauge (thickness) of the metal being slit.
- The slitting lines more often than not are positioned between running operations, being set up or readied for another pass.
- One machine is new and possesses a rotating turret for its cutters, allowing it to be set up for the next coil while the present one is slit.
- Raw material is purchased on the basis of actual or anticipated customer orders. Purchases for stock are minimal.
- Scheduling consists of matching orders, gauges, and materials to master coils. Sometimes, the material ordered is upgraded to fully utilize the master coil.
- One area contains "drops," or leftover portions of master coils used in fulfilling orders.
- Material handling is by forklift trucks, the normal payload of which is either a master coil or the finished coils produced from a master coil.
- A given order may utilize several pallets on which coils are mounted for shipment. The pallets are produced in an in-house sawmill.
- Certain customers' finished goods are stored until the customers request release.

The company's costing is based on the following traditional techniques:

- Material cost is specifically identified with coils used. Coil cost includes metal price and freight-in.
- Conversion costs including scrap, labor, and overhead are allocated among finished and drop coils on the basis of pounds. Weight represents the "equivalent unit."
- Drop coils consist of reusable material left after filling orders that is placed into storage for future use. The cost of drops includes a share of scrap like the costs for finished coils.

Within the framework for analysis just mentioned, the company is a hybrid of a manufacture-to-order and batch environment that utilizes a repetitive process. From a review of the activities, here are some of the issues in costing and in managing operations:

◆ Lot-based conversion and administrative costs, including order costs and setup, are highly significant to the operation. This calls into question the company's costing of small orders on the basis of weight alone.

◆ Drop coils represent a significant cost not applied to orders. When large quantities build up, they often have to be sold for scrap at a price that is less than their carrying cost. Costing must be questioned.

◆ Special services such as storage are not accounted for in costing.

These issues show a potentially significant distortion of costs and profits. Small orders are undercharged for conversion whereas large ones are overcharged. Unusual orders are undercharged for the drop material they generate and subsequent losses on disposal of drops are not charged. Nor are storage and other special services charged.

The resource usage path for Steel Service Company is shown in Exhibit 4-14. The supporting activities subject to level I assignment include supervision, maintenance, occupancy, personnel, employee benefits, and miscellaneous.

Some would argue that occupancy costs should be treated as discretionary and not assigned to products. But for Steel Service Company, space is meaningful for products because of a month-to-month lease arrangement on a portion of the plant. The costs would disappear if less space were consumed by operations or warehousing.

Discretionary Activities

Discretionary activities include:

◆ *Capacity decisions and bottlenecks.* Consistent with visibility in reporting, idle capacity and other capacity decisions should be segregated. Idle capacity includes discretionary downtime as well as fixed equipment costs not recovered through the normalized charge rate.

◆ *Abnormal scrap, rework.* These costs are directly charged to orders or customers as "special requirements" when incurred by them; whatever cannot be so charged is considered discretionary.

Exhibit 4-14. Resource Usage Path: Steel Service Company

Level I Drivers	Support Activities	Level II Drivers	Operating Activities	Costs
◆ Time, head count ◆ Square footage ◆ Head count ◆ Time and materials ◆ Vendors ◆ Asset value ◆ Value, remaining life ◆ Quantity consumed ◆ Head count, payroll dollars ◆ Related transactions	**Support** Supervision Occupancy Personnel Maintenance Purchasing Asset carrying costs Depreciation Utilities Payroll fringe Other administrative	◆ Discretionary	**Discretionary** Capacity decisions, bottlenecks Abnormal scrap, rework Nonmarket costs Cost of capital Training Advertising	**Resource Usage** End products Inventories Cost of sales Operating expenses
		◆ Orders ◆ Turret/other setups ◆ Footage, gauge ◆ Direct charge ◆ Master coils ◆ Pallets ◆ Asset value ◆ Direct charge ◆ Customers ◆ Products	**Direct** Order activities Slitting setup Slitting run Leftover material Material handling Packaging Asset carrying Expected scrap, rework Customer activities Tooling and design	
		◆ Specific customers, orders, products	**Special Requirements** Abnormal scrap, rework Expediting Non-normal tolerance Special packaging Special terms Miscellaneous services	

◆ *Cost of capital, owner salaries.* The mode of financing or level of officer compensation is not meaningfully applied at the product level. They are classified as discretionary.

◆ *Other discretionary.* The discretionary classification is relative to the significance of the items so labeled and the objectives of the ABM system. In a mail-order company, for example, advertising might be reclassified as an operating activity.

Direct Activities

Direct activities include:

◆ *Order activities.* Activities assigned to the orders activity driver include credit, purchasing, order processing, scheduling, and accounts receivable. Commissions are directly charged. Because it involves custom material, purchasing is based on customer orders received. The other relationships are largely self-explanatory.

◆ *Slitting setup.* The significance of setup is clear from the fact that slitting lines more often than not are between operations. Investigation of these costs and their drivers should be conducted. Assuming that setup alone accounts for most of the nondiscretionary time, the number of setups is the proper activity driver. A separate activity for turret setup is created because setup cost can be expected to decrease substantially. Setups may be actually tracked or based on the number of orders. If the latter, setup efficiencies gained by running similar orders will not be reflected in detailed estimating rates.

◆ *Slitting run.* While driven by footage, gauge also influences speed. Further classification into cost per foot according to light, medium, and heavy gauges may be sufficient. Otherwise, more activity drivers may be added. To budget footage, weight records maintained by gauge could be converted to footage using weight-per-foot factors. See Exhibit 4-15.

◆ *Leftover material.* Rather than being burdened with full costs, leftover or drop material should be marked to market reflected through a factor for likelihood of reutilization. In this manner, costs in excess of market value determined for these items are then assigned to the orders causing the cost.

◆ *Material handling.* Because the normal material-handling payload is either a master coil or the slitted output of one, and the distance traversed will total from one end to the other, master coils appear to be an appropriate driver. Master coils also include the reslitting of drop coils. Master

Exhibit 4-15. Derivation of Footage Activity Driver: Steel Service Company

Material, 36-Inch Width	Budgeted Weight	Conversion Factor	Budgeted Footage
Light-gauge	75,000,000	.2884	21,630,000
Medium-gauge	150,000,000	.1385	20,775,000
Heavy-gauge	200,000,000	.0577	11,540,000
	425,000,000		53,945,000

The purpose of this exhibit is to show how available information such as pounds may be readily converted into more meaningful bases like footage. The conversion factors derive from pounds per lineal foot of 36-inch-wide material divided into one.

and drop coils slit can be derived either from production or from material issue records.

◆ *Packaging.* Pallets as an activity driver is readily quantified from productivity reports of the in-house sawmill. Pallet making is combined with packaging because their activity drivers do not differ substantially.

◆ *Asset-carrying activities.* Inventory storage and accounts receivable payment terms have carrying costs in common, although the rates most likely differ. The rates can be determined with reference to financing or a required rate of return, plus specific costs associated with receivables and inventory activities. Carrying-cost rates are carrying costs divided by average asset levels.

◆ *Expected scrap and rework.* To the extent that these are anticipated from certain specifications, they become part of direct activity costing.

◆ *Customer activities.* This category includes customer service not appropriate to apply at the product level. The separate reporting of costs relating to large customers is intended to be used in reports analyzing profitability by customer.

◆ *Tooling, design, and product-line activities.* These costs are applied at the product level.

Special Requirements

Finally, special requirements reflect direct charges for all other significant customer requests, e.g., special packaging.

ABM answered management's need for information on off-fall. Further details are in the breakeven case in Chapter 11.

Machine Shop

MACHINE SHOP, INC.

Machine Shop, Inc., has all the information concerns generally associated with job shops. A widely varying output mix makes pricing and operational control difficult. The shop's single overhead rate is inadequate to reflect the varying complexity and machine intensity of its products. Management decides to try ABM.

Results: ABM provides the shop with needed information for pricing and operational control. With more effective costing, opportunities to improve efficiency and increase recovery of special requirements activities generate higher profits.

Machine shops manufacture a wide variety of custom products. Quoting and job costing are essential elements of the system. Layouts are based on function, whether it is milling, turning, or welding. Labor is relatively highly skilled. Setups are significant and frequent. Because jobs are unique, standardization of time spent may be difficult.

Technological advances include computer numerical control (CNC) machinery, under which setups may be programmed in advance. Once a fixture representing a setup configuration has been put into place, certain equipment may be able to run unattended.

A resource usage path for Machine Shop, Inc., is shown in Exhibit 4-16. Support, discretionary, and special requirements activities present no new issues. Because almost every order is highly customized, all production activities could be categorized as special requirements activities. But here, what is included as special are incremental items not included as direct activities, such as storing items on a customer's behalf.

Direct Activities

Direct activities are as follows:

   ◆ *Direct material and outside processing.* Direct material includes various metals in sheet, coil, or bar forms. Outside processing may include plating or other types of outsourced functions. As consistent with the

Exhibit 4-16. Resource Usage Path: Machine Shop

Level I Drivers	Support Activities	Level II Drivers	Operating Activities	Costs
◆ Time, head count ◆ Square footage ◆ Head count ◆ Time and materials ◆ Vendors, POs ◆ Asset value ◆ Value, remaining life ◆ Quantity consumed ◆ Head count, payroll dollars ◆ Related transactions	**Support** Supervision Occupancy Personnel Maintenance Purchasing Asset carrying costs Depreciation Utilities Payroll fringe Other administrative	◆ Discretionary	**Discretionary** Capacity decisions, bottlenecks Abnormal scrap, rework Marketing Cost of capital Nonmarket costs	**Resource Usage** End products Inventories Cost of sales Operating expenses
		◆ Direct charge ◆ Direct charge ◆ Orders ◆ Setups, time ◆ Cutting depth ◆ Parts, complexity ◆ Revolutions, travel ◆ Parts, complexity ◆ Direct charge ◆ Dies ◆ Weight, bulk	**Direct** Direct material, labor Engineering Order activities Setup (any activity) Turning Welding Hobbing Assembly CNC machining Tooling Shipping	
		◆ Specific customers, jobs	**Special Requirements** Customer-imposed capacity costs Abnormal scrap, rework Expediting Non-normal tolerance Special services	

nearly universal use of job-cost systems in the industry, material and out-side processing costs are charged to jobs directly. Care must be taken to ensure that off-fall generated is also charged.

♦ *Direct labor.* The direct labor category includes time spent per-forming machine shop operations. Under the job-cost system, labor is also directly charged to jobs. Assuming this continues under ABM, only over-head items would be assigned to jobs by means of activity drivers.

♦ *Engineering.* Engineering costs may be incurred in helping with cus-tomers' designs. Where significant, engineering time may be covered un-der the job-cost system by direct charge.

♦ *Order activities.* Order activities include production and general ad-ministrative functions associated with order scheduling, tracking, and, ultimately, accounting. Orders are the basis for assigning costs.

♦ *Turning.* The turning operation involves cutting a revolving work piece on a lathe. Setup, cutting depth, and units are factors for applying overhead related to tooling operations.

♦ *Welding.* Welding connects pieces of metal at their joints through heating. Setup, parts welded, and welds can be used for welding activity costs.

♦ *Hobbing.* Hobbing is a type of gear-cutting activity used to produce gears, sprockets, and wheels, among other items. The activity drivers in-clude number of hob revolutions and cutter travel.

♦ *Assembly.* Assembly pulls parts together into a final product. Driv-ers include number of parts and complexity.

♦ *CNC machining.* CNC machinery operates under the instructions of a computer program. As mentioned, CNC machinery significantly re-duces setup, so CNC setup must be distinguished from that of other ma-chines. Depending on the specific operation performed, machine time or part characteristics may be appropriate for assigning run costs.

♦ *Tooling design and maintenance.* Equipment requires tooling. Tooling for specialized customer applications is chargeable. Tooling costs gener-ally vary with the number of dies required to make the item. This can be tracked on a bill of activities.

♦ *Shipping.* Because of the diversity of items produced, a generic characteristic such as bulk or weight may be best for applying costs.

ABM proves to be well suited to the complex and varying output of the machine shop.

Metal Foundry

METAL FOUNDRY CO.

Metal Foundry Co. uses a traditional, single rate per labor hour for allocating conversion costs. After a new automated mold-and-pour line is installed alongside manual operations, management begins to question whether the company's costing method is still appropriate. It turns to ABM.

Results: Because of its significance, the new line becomes its own direct activity. Appropriate activity drivers are established for controlling the operation and assigning its costs to products.

Metal foundries produce metal castings from molten metal and molds using various casting techniques. While customer requirements vary significantly, the general routing is similar for all products.

Most foundries are small to medium-size job shops. As in other job-shop environments, laborers are highly skilled and attract above-average compensation. Automation is on the increase.

The gray iron foundry is the most typical example of a traditional foundry. With the increasing availability of low-cost competing materials, these foundries tend to develop niche markets encompassing complex designs. Their ability to customize and deliver on time often creates competitive advantages for them.

Product design heavily influences the efficiency and efficacy of the processes employed. Shapes are constrained to allow for workable stresses, solidification, and pattern removal. Cores made of fine sand can add complexity to shapes.

The traditional cost system typically used by such companies suffers from many common deficiencies. These include a labor-based, single overhead rate system (even though a new operation may have been added that is line-paced) and the fact that time incurred in different operations varies substantially by product. Moreover, overhead rates may be outdated, and order costs and special services may not be reflected in job profitability reporting.

The resource usage path for Metal Foundry Co. is shown in Exhibit 4-17. As with machine shops, the support, discretionary, and special requirements activities have been seen before. Maintenance costs in foundries are significant. If a work-order system is in place, costs not only are better controlled but can be charged directly to underlying activities.

Exhibit 4-17. Resource Usage Path: Metal Foundry

Level I Drivers	Support Activities	Level II Drivers	Operating Activities	Costs
	Support		**Discretionary**	**Resource Usage**
◆ Time, head count	Supervision	◆ Discretionary	Capacity decisions, bottlenecks	End products
◆ Square footage	Occupancy		Abnormal scrap, rework	Inventories
◆ Head count	Personnel		Marketing	Cost of sales
◆ Time and materials	Maintenance		Cost of capital	Operating expenses
◆ Vendors, POs	Purchasing		Nonmarket costs	
◆ Asset value	Asset carrying costs			
◆ Value, remaining life	Depreciation		**Direct**	
◆ Quantity consumed	Utilities	◆ Direct charge	Direct material	
◆ Head count, payroll dollars	Payroll fringe	◆ Orders	Order activities	
◆ Related transactions	Other administrative	◆ Weight, heat, time	Melt	
		◆ Cores, complexity	Core	
		◆ Molds	Mold	
		◆ Direct charge	Pattern	
		◆ Weights, molds	Pour	
		◆ Castings	Automated line	
		◆ Castings	Blast	
		◆ Castings, complexity	Grind	
		◆ Castings, complexity	Inspection	
		◆ Orders, castings	Shipping	
		◆ Size	Storage	
			Special Requirements	
		◆ Specific customers, jobs	Customer-imposed capacity costs	
			Abnormal scrap, rework	
			Expediting	
			Special services	

Direct Activities

Direct activities are as follows:

- *Direct material, core sand, and scrap.* Direct material includes scrap steel plate and coke, in a ratio of approximately 9:1. Weighing the metal charge in and out allows for direct charge of material as well as determination of yield and scrap. Core sand, which is generally expensive and non-recyclable, may also be directly charged by order.
- *Order activities.* For small runs, the costs of trial runs, setup operations, certain administrative costs, and shipping costs may be significantly higher. Run size may also affect choice of casting method, whether manual or automated. Costs associated with order activities are assigned to products using number of orders.
- *Melt.* Melt contributes significantly to total costs. The facilities are capital-intensive, requiring significant utility and maintenance costs. In addition to weight, operating time, heat level, and special-mix needs drive the costs. Yield may even be elevated into a key statistic.
- *Core.* Cores provide details to castings. Unlike the molds themselves, they are made from relatively expensive fine-grain sand that cannot be reused. Binding material and baking form the shape. Once the molten cast metal solidifies, the binder burns out, allowing the core mix to be poured from the casting.
- *Mold.* Molds are formed from patterns produced for customers. Green sand, the least expensive material, may be reused at a relatively high rate of recovery. Setup may account for over one quarter of total operating time.
- *Pattern.* As the patterns are billed to and owned by customers, pattern costs and associated services may be charged directly against their order. To the extent that storage and maintenance costs of patterns are significant, they may be assigned at a customer or order level.
- *Pour.* When the molds are ready, molten metal is transferred from the melt to the pouring areas; in the manual process, a ladle is used to fill the molds. Generally, costs of this activity are among the least significant to total.
- *Use automated mold-and-pour line.* Automated lines can combine molding and pouring activities. Whereas the manual operations are labor-paced, the automated operation is line-paced. Applying overhead on directly charged labor time is no longer applicable. Costs of the line and its crew are more properly spread over the output.

- *Blast.* Through sand blasting or hydraulics, the blast activity removes sand and scale from newly produced castings. If adjusted for a complexity factor, the number of castings could be used as a driver for this cost.

- *Grind.* Once blasted, castings are further refined through chipping or grinding to remove excess unwanted material. The intricacy of the design can heavily influence costs.

- *Inspect.* After cleaning, castings receive final inspection. Costs may be assigned on number of castings and adjusted for complexity. Rejection rates can vary substantially depending on design and level of experience with the items.

- *Ship.* Certain shipping costs are order- rather than unit-driven. Special packaging or expedited shipping are examples of services that should be directly charged.

- *Provide storage and interplant shipping.* Certain customers require storage, whereas others provide sufficient lead time for their orders to be produced during slow periods and shipped when needed. Interplant shipping charges should be highlighted as potentially avoidable through expansion of present space or relocation of a storage facility. In charging the costs, care needs to be taken to charge only those customers actually receiving the service for the costs. The remaining costs are discretionary and should be weighed against the savings of idle time.

Recognition of the unique aspects of the new line and other operating characteristics improves costing dramatically. With ABM, Metal Foundry Co.'s management has a basis for comparing the new and old processes.

5

Pinpointing Inefficiencies via ABM: Task-Oriented Operations under the Microscope

As should be readily apparent by now, ABM is able to uncover inefficiencies by showing how resources are consumed. This allows you to understand what causes costs. In the course of analysis, many inefficiencies will be exposed. The activity drivers indicate what is and isn't necessary to your operation, directing you toward optimizing the use of your resources.

All improvement programs start with information, which not only allows you to identify problems but enables you to measure and evaluate results. The key to identifying inefficiency and bringing hidden costs to light is to show the relationships between costs and their causes.

Now that you have the tools for identifying what's wrong with your operation, your next step is to decide what action to take. So many choices will become evident under ABM that you will need to prioritize. Therefore, to build momentum and support, first aim for sure-thing, large gains, and then move on to the next priority and so on as necessary. Activity drivers for activities you wish to target for cost reduction can become key statistics. When you elevate these to a high-profile level, you turn them into explicit statements of management objectives.

The two categories of inefficiency are:

1. Excessive resource consumption, caused by a workload that is higher than warranted by output
2. Capacity mismatched with workload

Reduction of Workload

The key to cutting costs and attaining efficiency is to decrease consumption of resources by reducing the quantity or cost of activity drivers. This frees up these resources for other uses. Actually, after implementing ABM, dealing with all the excess resources generated may in itself become a problem.

There are two subsets of cost-reduction opportunities:

1. Excessive number of activity drivers to produce a given output
2. Excessive cost per unit of activity driver

An example should clarify the relationship between the two.

MANUAL INFORMATION CO.

Manual Information Co. uses manual information systems. Accounting works with one set of numbers, operations with another, and sales with still another. Transactions are laboriously posted to journals, summarized, and finally entered into ledger books. The company needs to cost-justify a proposed integrated computer system. It applies ABM.

Results: ABM demonstrates that savings will be significant through a reduction of:

- *The number of times a transaction is entered* (by stopping the duplication of effort that leads to the excess)
- *The cost per transaction* (by eliminating the need to manually summarize and post the information)

The same is true about setup. One goal might be to reduce cost per occurrence; another, to reduce *number of* occurrences. Both reductions would decrease the demands placed on resources to produce a given level of output.

Redesign of the product, redesign of the process, and enhancement of efficiency all reduce the consumption of resources.

An age-old controversy rages around whether fractional workers, machines, or other resources can be saved. If certain parts of a resource cannot be terminated or sold, are so-called fractional savings possible? Since apparently the answer is yes, why not make them? If your company takes the extreme view that only whole resources should be pursued, you may find it difficult to suggest fractional improvements, especially if it's your job that's on the line. "Whole resource" savings constraints tend to make individual effort at improvements almost impossible.

RULE OF THUMB: FRACTIONAL RESOURCE SAVING

When contemplating fractional resource savings, the only way to reach a satisfactory solution is to consider capacity. What resources once occupied with inefficiency can now be used elsewhere? Can Joe now use the two freed-up hours to perform preventive maintenance, study setups, or attend to the hundred-odd other projects that he formerly did not have time to consider? Ultimately, combining functions may be possible.

Actions for Reducing Workload

Seventeen action ideas for reducing workload are outlined in Exhibit 5-1 and explained in the following sections.

1: Analyze Activities

Because almost every business has one area—administration—in common, let's start there. You may gather some action ideas that will help you in your operation.

Ferreting out inefficiency in administrative functions starts by understanding activities, their costs, and their causes. Once the model of your operation is complete, you can easily identify wasteful areas and cut costs.

To control these costs, identify the drivers that best reflect what causes them. A substantial portion of general and administrative functions, such as accounting, data processing, and clerical tasks, is "variable," or responsive to volume changes. For example, a billing activity can be connected to the number of invoices, check writing to the number of checks, and so on. Where these activities are individually insignificant, they may be aggregated and applied according to the number of customer orders or some other reasonable basis.

Activity drivers for administration might include:

+ *Output measures*—e.g., pages copied or words typed.
+ *Transaction measures*—e.g., number of surprise customer requests, pieces of correspondence.

Exhibit 5-1. Seventeen Action Ideas for Reducing Workload

1. Analyze activities.	10. Monitor quality costs.
2. Target outputs.	11. Recognize carrying costs.
3. Eliminate duplication.	12. Truncate unnecessary handling.
4. Remove downtime.	13. Track marketing and advertising.
5. Break system constraints.	14. Attain lot-level efficiencies.
6. Match activities with resources.	15. Avoid overautomating.
7. Centralize activities.	16. Focus on scrap.
8. Capture customer costs.	17. Investigate shrinkage.
9. Eradicate rework.	

- *Time measures*—e.g., a five-week backlog of unbilled invoices, which has implications for receivables carrying costs.
- *Special requirements*—exceptions to procedures for certain customers, which is likely to cause a large increase in processing time.

Many professional firms have already realized that in today's competitive environments, it is even more critical to take this area seriously.

PROFESSIONAL FIRM ADMINISTRATIVE STAFF

While practically unheard of in the past, many professional firms now require time reporting from their administrative as well as professional staffs. Although it is not necessary to require accountability to that degree, analysis of activities and their drivers is still needed to control administrative costs.

Results: There is better monitoring of administrative functions, and improvement in capacity planning, efficiency, and accuracy of special customer requirements costing.

2: Target Outputs

Unnecessary reports are a favorite target of ABM. Electronic data interchange (EDI) lets you get rid of a lot of paper. EDI tracks purchase orders, receipts, and accounts payable electronically. The same is true for bar coding.

Additional costs often result from unplanned activities. If unscheduled orders are creating problems, perhaps recognizing the true cost will motivate the sales department to obtain forecasted requirements or blanket orders from customers.

3: Eliminate Duplication

The case study for Manual Information Co. discussed a few pages back shows how unnecessary—and costly—duplication can occur when systems are not integrated. At Manual, each department has its own data processing staff to generate management information. The sales department enters orders to track customer activity; operations enters the same orders to provide processing instructions; and finally, accounting enters the orders once again for invoicing. Obviously, it is more efficient to enter the information once in such a way that all three areas can draw upon it.

4: Remove Downtime

An extremely useful exercise in setting up an ABM system is to measure output in relation to practical capability. If a machine can produce 10,000 invoices a day but on average turns out only 2,000, what is happening the remaining 80 percent of the time?

A type of downtime becoming common everywhere results from time saved by operating a computer instead of waiting for a process to run. The resultant downtime may represent 30 percent or more a day. Considering the high skill levels involved, this issue is especially disturbing.

GRAPHIC ARTS CO.

While implementing ABM, it is discovered that operator time charged to similar projects varies substantially, depending upon the number of personal computers available. When fewer operators are present, those who *are* there tend to be more productive. Investigation reveals that an operator can better utilize a computer when two PCs are available. Then, he or she can work on several jobs at once.

Results: By weighing the costs under ABM, management finds several acceptable, low-cost ways to improve operators' efficiency and productivity.

 ◆ Implementing a file server, to eliminate the idle processing time lag for operators
 ◆ Dedicating a workstation to performing run tasks only
 ◆ Where run-time requirements are predictable, assigning more than one computer to an operator

Consequent time savings translate into substantial dollars.

This scenario also occurs in machine-paced manufacturing operations. Press operation may account for under 30 percent and slitting operations for under 40 percent of an operator's day. What accounts for the remaining 60 or 70 percent? And what portion of nonproductive activities is avoidable through process, design, or other improvements? To determine the answer, production reporting systems should analyze downtime statistics by cause each day.

Direct labor may waste time waiting for material, instructions, or repair of breakdowns. Better communication of instructions or scheduling around problems can cut the waste. Breakdowns can be avoided through planning, the use of preventive maintenance programs, or optimizing tool replacement. If performed by a specially designated team or by less than a full operator crew, setup may also result in downtime. These topics are treated in detail in the discussion of lot-level efficiencies later in this chapter.

Tightening the process may also reduce costs, as shown by the following case study.

COIL FINISHING CO. OPERATION

ABM has identified certain inefficiencies in coil-driven costs. After the setup has been completed, one crew, apparently oblivious to the arm provided on the metals machine for storing the next coil, habitually loads a new coil. Management decides to act upon the ABM information.

Results: Once the crew learns to signal for the coil in advance, the reduced waiting time becomes apparent.

Depending on the process, another cause of downtime may be poor quality of material. If caused internally, this cost should be separately designated as a quality cost. If caused by a vendor, a different response is called for.

EVALUATING METALS VENDORS

At Coil Finishing Co., a single weld in a coil can cause twenty minutes of downtime. Although operations has identified the vendors responsible for the substandard quality, purchasing, seeking low price, continues to buy from them.

Results: Once ABM is implemented, operations can quantify what the low-quality material *really* costs the company. More important, by involving all functions in the implementation, ABM helps operations overcome the communications barrier.

Realizing that costs of poor quality should be considered when selecting suppliers, purchasing develops a system for evaluating and rating suppliers to ensure that criteria other than price are considered in buying decisions. The actual savings achieved well exceeds vendor price differentials.

5: Break System Constraints

Like downtime, a system may impose other constraints. The process may be overly complex, or it may be weighed down by bureaucracy. Or an information system may not be well-suited for its use. Take the following case.

AUTOMATED INEFFICIENCY

While analyzing transaction processing under ABM, it is discovered that for certain functions, inputting a single data element takes as long as inputting twenty. Upon investigation, the cause turns out to be the computer system, which requires the same ten screens to be traversed no matter what is being input.

Results: Management decides to modify the computer system to better suit the use for which it is intended. For minor data updates, excess screens are programmed out.

6: Match Activities with Resources

One form of waste occurs when specially skilled employees perform tasks below their skill level—e.g., when an attorney performs paralegal tasks or a registered nurse performs the duties of a nurse's aide.

Reassigning routine tasks to employees at a lower skill level frees up capacity of skills. Where possible, certain of these low-skill tasks may be automated.

Another form of waste occurs where a high-quality (and more costly) part/material is substituted for a lower-quality one. This may be appropriate when the lower-quality part is unavailable, but the practice should be monitored and controlled through an authorization procedure to make sure it is not abused.

STEEL COMPANY

While implementing ABM, Steel Company makes a startling discovery about its sophisticated (but traditional) cost system. Under its standards, cost accounting posts the cost of a frequent substitution of a high-cost item for a low-cost one to a miscellaneous variance account called "facility mix." But for product profitability analyses, the sales are costed out at the standard, unsubstituted material price. As it happens, use of the actual price turns the apparent margin for the product into a loss.

Results: The managers not only change the accounting treatment but also prohibit the material substitution, thus stopping the hidden bleeding.

Utilizing an expensive machine with special capabilities does not make sense when a general-purpose machine will do. Similarly, when special skills are required in moving certain types of items, capacity of those skills should match the need.

7: Centralize Activities

An idea similar to matching activities to resources is centralization. Tasks become "skilled"; machines become "dedicated." Quality becomes more uniform and standardization improves. Unlike specialists, people who perform tasks infrequently are likely to spend much more time doing them. Similarly, dedicated machines avoid adjustments needed for running other work.

8: Capture Customer Costs

Certain customers may require special services, for which they are not charged—e.g., when a full-time customer service representative has to deal with a major customer every day or when special reports or projects are requested. "Loss leader" product costs are also caused by customers. Other customers may simply be a nuisance.

To reduce or eliminate them, these costs *must* be captured in the ABM system. An entire section of the resource usage path, you'll recall, is dedicated to these special requirements activities. The results of analysis may influence pricing (as covered in Chapter 8).

9: Eradicate Rework

Rework arises from work done incorrectly the first time. According to W. Edwards Deming's well-known 40/30/30 rule, defects are attributable 40 percent to design, 30 percent to process, and 30 percent to vendors. For example, foundries build in scrap and rework factors when bidding on complex items, because a certain level of failure is inherent in the design. These costs should be charged to the order causing them.

Technology can improve quality and standardization and decrease rework. A process may be made fail-safe so that it cannot produce bad items. At a lesser extreme, automation may reduce rework.

BAR CODING

Data input may average three errors per thousand characters input. If the errors are caught upon review, correction requires rework. If they are not, the consequences may be much more dramatic: An important shipment may go out wrong or not go at all; an essential raw material may not be ordered; an important customer may be lost. ABM can assist in weighing the costs and benefits of alternative technologies, such as bar coding.

Results: If rework and related costs are high, bar coding, which reduces the possibility of error, becomes viable. Rework and other costs then cease to be an issue.

For rework that isn't chargeable, a companywide effort may be called for to ensure eradication. Specific causes must be formally documented as attributable to design flaws, process inadequacies, or particular vendors. But for a companywide effort to be effective, the costs must first be made visible.

For example, in a gray iron foundry, items for rework or scrap may be identified as having certain physical characteristics, including cracked or scabbed mold, sand or slag in the iron, dirty or collapsed core, too little iron poured, or too much grinding. Further investigation may trace the problem to a particular molding line or untrained coremaker.

10: Monitor the Costs of Quality

Costs of quality include controls for preventing and detecting defects, and the consequences of what happens when those controls fail. Prevention includes the additional design and engineering effort used to improve process and product design. Detection includes the traditional inspection function, and the related corrections or rework performed. Consequences would include the cost of receiving, processing, and disposing of returned merchandise. Some of the failure costs, such as lost customer goodwill, are of course intangible.

Strangely enough, some companies pursue a zero-defect policy by 100 percent inspection and reinspection of output. Strange, because inspection after the fact is unnecessary if quality is ensured within a process. In a controlled process, operator sampling of output by such techniques as statistical process control should be sufficient.

11: Recognize Carrying Costs

Extending credit to customers is an investment in accounts receivable. This investment is worth making only if the resulting incremental sales outweigh the associated carrying costs. These include the opportunity costs of tied-up capital, financing, credit approval functions, collection costs, and bad-debt write-offs. Costs associated with carrying assets should be so categorized.

GAMES DISTRIBUTOR CO.

Games Distributor Co. has a problem with accounts receivable. Its turnover rate is approximately three times per year, compared with an industry average of six. In the process of weighing alternatives, the company turns to ABM.

Results: The company determines what the low turnover rate is really costing. Collections average $100,000 per day. Considering the interest costs alone, the annual savings on its working capital loan with a 10 percent interest rate from accelerating collections by just one day amount to $10,000. Having attached a number to the potential savings, the benefits are weighed against costs of alternate collection techniques, such as prompt payment discounts or use of a lockbox for timely crediting of deposits.

Like accounts receivable, inventory balances represent an investment that demands return to offset its costs. Costs include those for personal property taxes, insurance, warehousing, handling, shrinkage, and obsolescence. Work-in-process levels measure manufacturing lead times, reduction of which not only reduces carrying costs but improves flexibility and customer satisfaction.

For products spending substantial time in queues either because they require cooling or simply due to a high level of work in process in the plant, try a daily carrying rate. That rate should be related to this category of expenses through flexible budgeting.

Not all output should be burdened with carrying costs. When goods become finished, another set of rules may apply.

MANUFACTURING AND STORAGE CO.

Manufacturing and Storage Co. maintains a warehouse for finished goods, the costs of which are averaged over all products. However, it is found that only certain customers require the warehousing; the remaining space holds slow-moving products.

Results: After correcting the cost system, management institutes a storage charge for its customers. Customers who no longer get the service free are likely to reconsider whether they really need it. Management also reexamines the need for carrying the slow-moving inventory. The ultimate result is reduced warehousing costs overall.

12: Truncate Unnecessary Handling

Like downtime, material-handling costs should be highlighted separately. Material handling has been the object of attacks lately. It is considered a **non-value-added** activity, since moving parts from point A to point B does nothing to improve those parts.

Unnecessary material handling is not limited to manufacturing environments. Accounting may spend inordinate amounts of time—e.g., tracking down paper to find out when something was ordered, paid, or received, or needlessly going to files for information that's available on the computer—making up for information system deficiencies. These activities definitely do not add value.

ABUNDANT MATERIALS, INC.

Abundant Materials, Inc., determines through ABM that it spends too much of its resources on material handling. Its activity drivers include:

- ◆ Distance moved
- ◆ Number of times issued (i.e., unnecessary paperwork)
- ◆ Idle vehicle capacity (determined in a way similar to that described for machinery in the discussion of downtime)

Management investigates these causes further.

Results: Management takes the following actions to reduce the activity drivers identified—and hence, the costs:

- Reconfigure shop-floor layout and storage areas to minimize distance moved. The most used items are now stored on the shop floor or placed in the most accessible areas.
- Reduce the number of issues by eliminating the practice of restocking and issuing subassemblies during production.
- Install a preventive maintenance program to cure excess vehicle capacity resulting from excessive breakdown time. The extra vehicles are sold for cash.

Excess capacity may be chargeable to certain customers or products. For example, metals operations requiring a lift truck to load and unload may vary significantly in running time. From a study of one operation in particular, average utilization was found to be approximately 65 percent of capacity, if 100 percent was assumed to be all quick-run time items. In such a situation, it may be most equitable to charge the excess capacity to the quick-run items that cause the need for the capacity.

13: Track Marketing and Advertising

Advertising expenditures are sometimes insignificant. They may be adequately evaluated by dividing costs by the percentage profit contributed by sales generated. The profit contribution represents selling price less the cost of the additional activities required to fill orders. To illustrate, at a selling price of $100 and a profit of $40, the percentage profit is 40 percent. An advertising expenditure of $100,000 must then generate at least $250,000 in sales revenue to pay for itself.

However, certain industries need a much more detailed analysis of marketing and advertising activities, and so may choose to classify them as direct, rather than discretionary, activities. For example, mail order companies, who depend on extensive and diverse forms of advertising for their revenue, may need to track details of the number of inquiries and sales from the various media sources. A key statistic for ABM in companies selling by mail on installments might be collection by customer by medium, allowing them to concentrate their efforts on the most profitable audiences.

14: *Attain Lot-Level Efficiencies*

The following action ideas relate to so-called lot-level costs, introduced in Chapter 3. Certain costs, like setup, are incurred with the number of lots produced, not the number of units. Similar costs are those incurred by the order, whether sale or purchase.

In the administrative function, order costs are a form of lot-based costs incurred per order regardless of size. Such costs include order processing, credit approval, scheduling, production reporting, costing, billing, accounts receivable maintenance, and collection.

The action ideas presented here have wide application.

Machine Setup   Machine setup is a prime example of a lot-based cost, as it occurs only between lots of distinct parts. ABM provides separate accounting for these costs, which may have been treated in various ways previously.

METALS OPERATION CO.

Metals Operation Co. bases its product costing on actual machine time to run, plus a percentage of that time for setup cost. Setup costs charged are proportionate to run time, meaning a large lot incurs more setup cost than a small one, even if the items produced are identical. Management cannot obtain true small-order cost information, necessary for minimum-order limits, from the cost system. Management likewise does not know the profitability of small runs. For answers, it turns to ABM.

Results: Under ABM, machine setup becomes a separate activity from run. Whereas run costing comes from a measure of output, setup cost is based on number of lots set up, or setup time if types vary. Management is able to obtain the information necessary to assess small-order profitability and establish minimum-order limits.

To maximize flexibility, increase capacity, and minimize cost, manufacturers should monitor setup time and methods for potential reduction. As far as possible, operations for the next lot should be set up while the current lot is running. For certain coil-processing operations, rotating turrets may make this possible. For other machines, dedicated tools or fixtures might allow this. In addition to detailed videotape analysis of crews involved, other increasingly popular ways of reducing setup include utilization of computer-numerical-control machinery and implementation of group technology. Other improvements may be made by something as simple as organizing tools and settings.

Lot Sizing   Because ABM precisely quantifies setup cost, better information is available for use in assessing lot-sizing trade-offs. Cost per purchase order is comparable to setup but applies to purchased instead of manufactured items. Under the economic order quantity (EOQ) formula, the optimal lot size is determined by minimizing order costs (setup and purchase) and carrying costs. The formula is as follows:

$$EOQ = \text{Square root of } [(2 \times U \times O)/(I \times C)],$$

where variables are defined as:

   U Usage per year
   O Order cost
   I Item cost
   C Carrying cost, expressed as a percentage rate per year

For example, one company produces small zinc castings. Under a policy of lot-size reduction, it had set a maximum of 15 pieces, which meant that because of process limitations, generally 18 pieces had to be poured. Assuming raw material cost of $1 per casting, a weekly use of 15 pieces, carrying costs averaging 20 percent, zero scrap recovery, and no setup cost other than $3 in rejected pieces, the formula indicates:

$$EOQ = \text{Square root of } [(2 \times (52 \times 15) \times \$3]/[\$1 \times 20\%] = 153$$

With a quantity of 153, carrying costs are 20 percent of the average inventory on hand of 77 pieces (half the order quantity), or $15. Likewise, order costs are $3 each times the number of orders, calculated as 52 times 15 or 780 divided by 153, or 5. Five orders times $3 likewise is $15, for a total annual cost of $30.

Compare this to a lot size of 15. Carrying costs drop substantially, from $15 to $2, or 8 pieces times 20 percent. Order costs, however, more than make up for the savings. Instead of $15 per year, order costs of $3 are applied on 52 orders (780/15) for a cost of $156. Total costs are $158.

Assuming the underlying data and assumptions of EOQ are valid in this situation, the company would save 80 percent of total ordering and carrying costs. Spread across the entire castings product line, the savings quickly add up.

Some companies, on the other hand, attempt to live with the setup constraint differently. In seasonal environments, specialized, short-run items are reserved for the off season. While this is one way of coping with the problem, it is better to tackle the problem and free up the off-season capacity for more productive endeavors.

Finally, like any order point method, EOQ should be applied only to items subject to external demands, such as end products or service parts. If component parts are ordered through a reorder point model, the level of various components will not balance in the form of number of end items producible, and the level of inventory will be higher than necessary. For manufacturing components, material requirements planning (MRP) is the appropriate solution. This explodes forecasts of end items through bills of material into time-phased component-order requirements. Also, EOQ should not be applied indiscriminately to items subject to varying external demand. For example, if a reorder point for snow shovels is tripped at the end of March, an order at that time means carrying them until the next year!

Tooling Optimization   Tooling replacement decisions are a classic example of planning in maintenance. Downtime and the run interruption that occurs from the need to replace worn tooling could be minimized by using standard tool replacement formulae. This is lot-based efficiency because the timing must be optimized within lot-size constraints. A classic equation used in engineering, for example, is:

Tool life (minutes) to minimize cost = R (1/F -1),

where:

$$R = (A + B)/T,$$

and variables are defined as:

A Cost to change and adjust a tool after an edge has worn out
B Cost of replacing the tool or reconditioning its cutting edge
T The average operating cost per minute of machine and operator including overhead
F Tool life/cutting speed factor

For example, starting with the costs required for *A* and *B*, say a tool costs $15 and takes 20 minutes to replace at a cost of $1.20 per minute. The total cost involved with tool change (*A* + *B*) is $39. To convert these costs into time, divide by *T*, which was defined as $1.20 per minute. The result is 32.5 equivalent minutes of cost. The factor (*F*) is available in engineering reference manuals. If *F* is assumed to be .35, the second half of the equation becomes 1.86. Multiplying this by 32.5 minutes results in an optimum tool life of 60 minutes.

While the equation is time-based, it can easily be adapted to output or cost-driver measures by stating either of them in terms of time as well. If the machine speed is 50 units per minute, optimal life is 3,000 units. For a lot size of 2,500 units, it becomes clear that the tool should be replaced between each lot.

Similarly, a preventive maintenance program may include the use of nonoperating periods in which to perform maintenance tasks so that machines are ready for use when needed in operations. Certain industries may opt for periodic complete shutdowns for maintenance. These shutdowns may prevent delays that would otherwise idle workers and destroy sales.

15: Avoid Overautomating

Because of the assumption that costs follow labor, line managers who still use traditional systems may seek to replace labor with equipment. All too often, however, automation may be the wrong choice, as the following examples illustrate:

• Automation of one operation may create bottlenecks for others, limiting the increase in productivity. **Bottlenecks** are operations that constrain others because of insufficient capacity.

• You may be replacing low-cost hourly labor with skilled maintenance personnel. It may then be necessary to increase control over maintenance and related costs, requiring a work-order system.

• Too often, automation of material handling or other functions is undertaken to reduce nonoperation time, without sufficient study of the portion of the time actually affected.

• A shockingly dangerous situation may arise when purchasing new technology or automating a new operation not previously in house: assuming that excess capacity can be used to produce items readily saleable to external customers. Unfortunately, fixed overhead and debt obligations remain even when an asset is idle. More about this in the discussion about adjusting capacity.

ABM's method for analyzing capital expenditure decisions is covered in Chapter 7.

16: Focus on Scrap

As with downtime and rework, you should set up a reporting system to make sure that the causes of scrap are reported and investigated. Scrap reports should include not only quantities but specific circumstances, such as those discussed in the section on rework. Acting on the causes ensures future efficiency. Those situations that are correctable will then not continue to bleed the operation. To enhance recovery, further processing of scrap (e.g., sorting or baling) should be considered. Reusable scrap items should be available in a single designated area to facilitate usage.

Special valuation problems arise with leftover, drop, or off-fall material consisting of items that may potentially be applied to another order.

A common example is material left over from metal-cutting operations. At one extreme, this material could be fully burdened with conversion costs as if it were finished goods. At the other, it could be assigned only scrap value. The solution probably lies between these extremes. If it is unlikely that the material will be reused, assigning it to scrap value is appropriate. Otherwise, it should be assigned a fraction of the metal cost, representing reuse probability. Any loss in value of the leftover piece would be properly chargeable to the customer order that generated it.

17: Investigate Shrinkage

Much of what has been discussed regarding cost control presumes that a good inventory control system is in place to prevent and, when necessary, promptly detect shrinkage. Elements of a good control system include perpetual records, restricted access, assigned responsibility, and formal authorization for requisitions. This does not imply that costing and accounting must be complex. Backflushing, for example, is a technique by which inventory is relieved through bill of material explosion at the point an item is completed or shipped—which, in some situations, may be all that is needed.

Adjustment of Capacity

Why does ABM highlight the effects of **capacity decisions** as discretionary activities? As you may have surmised, ABM's segregation and analysis of discretionary costs is a major part of improving operations. For efficiency, analyses should be made of overtime, downtime, rework, and skills applied. Causes of problems must be documented and fully communicated.

Certain costs, including overtime and rework, may be categorized as "discretionary" or "waste" to the extent that they are not expected to occur in routine operations. Portions that are expected to occur should be charged to a specific customer order or product. Under ABM, this distinction should be scrupulously adhered to when determining the costs of sales. For example, customer costs for overtime caused by expediting an order, or rework created by providing an overly complex specification, should be charged to that customer. On the other hand, general overtime or occasional rework may be related to management policy or other factors and, as such, should be segregated from the costs of other operating activities in analysis.

While recognizing conflicting objectives, ABM allows for explicit trade-offs by providing the means to compare costs of alternatives. Keep in mind that there are no absolutes when it comes to improving efficiency. The old school of manufacturing solved the problem of idle time by keeping workers busy. No one foresaw that carrying costs on slow-moving inventory would create their own operating problems. Now because of the bitter experience of being choked by excess inventory investment, it is clear that idle time, while never desirable, may save the company money by costing the company less than carrying excess inventory. ABM permits separate, visible reporting of downtime and costs of carrying inventory so that the optimal solution may be chosen.

The first problem you are likely to encounter when resources are freed up through ABM is potential excess capacity. Optimally, any excess capacity should be redeployed to growth areas. Otherwise, you may be faced with poor morale, limiting ABM's success. Optimally, the goal is to match capacity with necessary workload. Deviation results in costs that should be highlighted for corrective action.

Too Much Capacity

Downtime caused by a lack of work is a discretionary cost representing available capacity that should be separately reported and recognized in accounting records. A classic example of overstaffing is the once-fashionable practice of having a secretary for each executive. All too often, the practice could not be justified from the point of view of either efficiency or workload. Replacing personal secretaries with reception staffs and typing pools allowed for more efficient specialization, more standardization in output, and better control over capacity. The result was considerable cost savings.

Excess equipment capacity should be reported and recognized in the same way. Too often, we tend to pool extra equipment costs so that they are spread over all the machines, resulting in the overcosting of high-volume machine output. This creates the risk that orders will be lost. A landlord cannot consider excess capacity in setting rents. It would be futile to attempt to recapture the cost of an entire building through charges to a single tenant. As described in Chapter 3, ABM treatment entails the separate calculation of a budget of activity, e.g., costs applied to orders, on the basis of normal volume. Remaining unabsorbed costs are charged to idle capacity.

In some respects, the costs of slow-turning inventories to service customers may be considered capacity costs. As with other costs of over-capacity, you must weigh the costs and benefits of a given strategy.

Too Little Capacity

Unless chargeable to a specific customer, overtime occurs at the discretion of management. Along with its specifying causes, overtime should be separately identified in reporting so that when they note excessive overtime, managers can see the explanation immediately.

HABITUAL OVERTIME CO.

Habitual Overtime Co. has a problem with (you guessed it!) habitual overtime. Employees seem to create any number of excuses for coming in after hours for extra pay. Management implements an ABM reporting system that highlights these costs as discretionary in reporting and documentation of causes.

Results: With this information, management soon recognizes that overtime is a problem of significant magnitude; its causes as reported are trivial. Management takes immediate steps to curb the problem, including:

- ◆ Initiating a standard operating procedure that discourages overtime
- ◆ Requiring responsible supervisors to approve overtime in writing in advance
- ◆ Setting limits on overtime per employee per period

But reporting may also indicate that personal spending money is not the only cause of overtime. Workers may have to make up for production delays arising from machine breakdowns. This may prod shocked managers to reconsider proposals for comprehensive preventive maintenance. If fewer breakdowns occur, there will be less overtime.

What are the advantages of paying overtime over hiring more people? With ABM, you can compare the costs of hiring and training new employees (including the costs of medical insurance and certain payroll taxes) with the overtime alternative. The balance between the two costs represents the net cost impact of the decision.

Costs arising from undercapacity also occur in other areas. Too little material resources may cause the need for expediting orders to vendors, resulting in added costs. Work centers themselves may become bottlenecks. Tracking and controlling queues at these operations become essential. When bottlenecks are attributable to certain customers or products, they should become chargeable rather than discretionary.

Matching capacity and workload is a constant management challenge. Ultimately, if customers must be turned away, there may be a loss of business.

Monitoring Capacity

Capacity monitoring does not call for time reporting. It can be regulated just as effectively by using activity drivers to gauge workloads, as the following example from a chain of beauty clinics illustrates.

BEAUTYUSA

Because it is impossible to predict the number or timing of customer visits, capacity planning for BeautyUSA (a chain of beauty clinics) is crucial. Without timely indicators of performance, corporate management is powerless to maintain control, since it has no information until the end of the month when monthly financial statements are issued. It needs a key statistic to allow for more frequent monitoring and goal setting.

Results: After implementing ABM, BeautyUSA uses the ratio of technician hours (capacity) to treatments (workload) to benchmark performance and determine staff utilization. What becomes readily apparent from tracking the indicator is trends toward overstaffing relative to local markets (see Exhibit 5-2).

Compared to location A, with the highest ratio, location C's staff appears to be only half utilized. Resources do not appear to be well matched with the local market. With these statistics available every pay period,

Exhibit 5-2. Staffing Performance: BeautyUSA

WEEKLY REPORT

Clinic	Treatments	Technicians	Ratio
Location A	195	2	98
Location B	345	4	86
Location C	211	4	53
Location D	157	2	79
Location E	251	3	84

Predicting local capacity needs is critical when staffing a chain of beauty clinics. Treatments per technician may provide a key indicator through which performance can be assessed. Certain situations may call for immediate attention. For instance, why is location C not performing?

management can react to changes in market conditions more quickly. The result is more profitable operations.

Practical Pointers

♦ Although the discussion presented here may seem extensive, it covers only a fraction of the inefficiency typically identified during ABM implementation. Because each operation is unique, it is impossible to anticipate each area of inefficiency that can be disclosed. This chapter only provides a starting point.

♦ With operations under control, ABM information can be applied in other areas. The microlevel discussion covered here has macrolevel consequences, as discussed in the next chapter.

6

Honing In
on the True Costs
of Activities

Until now, we have focused on the details of using information generated by ABM. Now let's step back to look at the big picture—the impact of ABM on assessing the company as a whole and measuring profitability by significant area.

Using Activity Drivers

Once determined, the information provided by activity drivers can be looked at from nearly any viewpoint desired. Say your operation contains two supporting activities and two direct activities. Their drivers are designated as S-1, S-2 and D-1, D-2, respectively. Each activity occurs 100 times during a specified period. Consider the following analysis by product line:

| | Activity Driver Quantity | |
Activity Driver	Product A	Product B
S-1	50	50
S-2	70	30
D-1	0	100
D-2	80	20

By applying costs per unit of driver and comparing them to sales information, you might get these results:

Activity Driver	Cost per Driver	Extended Driver Quantity	
		Product A	Product B
Sales		$1,000	$1,000
Costs			
S-1	$4	200	200
S-2	$5	350	150
D-1	$1	0	100
D-2	$8	640	160
		1,160	610
Net profit (loss)		($160)	$390
Percentage		(16%)	39%

You can arrange activity drivers according to any meaningful category. Consider the following examples:

By department:

Activity Driver	Activity Driver Quantity	
	Department A	Department B
S-1	30	70

By customer:

Activity Driver	Activity Driver Quantity	
	Product A	Product B
S-1	60	40

By customer annual sales volume:

Activity Driver	Activity Driver Quantity	
	Over $100,000	Under $100,000
S-1	35	65

By location:

	Activity Driver Quantity	
Activity Driver	*Location A*	*Location B*
S-1	55	45

By marketing channel:

	Activity Driver Quantity	
Activity Driver	*Channel A*	*Channel B*
S-1	90	10

By salesperson:

	Activity Driver Quantity	
Activity Driver	*Salesperson A*	*Salesperson B*
S-1	40	60

By vendor:

	Activity Driver Quantity	
Activity Driver	*Product A*	*Product B*
S-1	70	30

And so on. The type of ABM report you use is up to you. For example, a collection agency might want to view costs in different ways. Its two major activities, drivers, and cost rates are as follows:

Activity ("Cost")	*Driver ("Cause")*	*Cost per Driver*
Contact debtor	Number of contacts	$3.50
Administer item	Number of items	$10.00

Using this information, profitability reports could compare the following:

- ◆ Commercial as opposed to retail collections
- ◆ Small as opposed to large commercial debtors
- ◆ Profitability by customer
- ◆ Profitability by age of debt (time outstanding)
- ◆ Profitability by debt amount

If the contacts average three per collection, it is unlikely that the agency will accept debts under $20. Administration alone would cost $10, plus contact activities of $10.50.

Examples of ABM in Action

Performing analyses by customer, business location, distribution channel, and product line is nothing new. What is new is how these analyses are done according to ABM. Whereas traditional techniques rely on averaging and "allocations," analysis under ABM, with its detailed cost assignments, provides you with insight into the niche markets most profitable to your business.

Let's compare ABM and a traditional report for a company engaged in two distinct lines of business.

Repair Shop

Many companies engage in diverse lines of business that call for adequate accounting. A dealer in new boats may also have a retail shop for accessories. A distributor may sell products as well as offer rental arrangements. A manufacturer may choose to act as its own distributor or even retailer.

A company with two or more distinct lines of business under the same roof needs a way to evaluate each. Would each business be able to survive on its own? Which business should be emphasized and which cut back? The example presented here is of a repair shop for electric motors that also functions as a distributor.

Traditional accounting says that if the line of business makes a contribution toward corporate selling, general, and administrative overhead (which is considered "fixed"), that business should continue. This evades direct answers to the questions managers may ask about controlling costs. The exhibits detailing costs for an electric motor shop will hopefully clarify how ABM can better address the issue of assigning general overhead to specific lines of business.

Managers of shops that both repair and distribute motors find that in some ways, the two endeavors are in conflict: Improvements in electric motor technology have reduced the need for repairs; some new motors sold on the distribution side are now so inexpensive that they have become "throwaways"; and the once overlapping specialty of crediting customers for trade-ins of old motors is waning. These are all circumstances that may indicate a change of strategy over the long term.

Because of increasing competition, repair customers now require quotes of turnaround time and price before allowing shops to commence work, which requires a detailed estimating system along the lines to be described in Chapter 8. The optimal information system would integrate quoting with purchasing, ordering, receiving, inventory, customer charges, invoicing, and accounts payable processing.

Turnaround time is an essential benchmark. To achieve the shortest turnaround time, repair services must balance operations performed internally against farmed-out stock on hand or merchandise ordered from vendors and must weigh high shop capacity against low.

These repair services must base their make-or-buy decisions on asset utilization; general-purpose machining equipment is preferred to the highly specialized. Where infrequent operations or repair needs do not provide enough volume to justify insourcing, the repair shops need to seek vendors whose competitive advantage is in timely turnaround and delivery, price alone being an inappropriate criterion. Internally, certain assets, such as armature-rewinding machines, are essential but expected to be less than fully utilized. Costing of less-utilized assets should reflect an assumption of normal volume for applying fixed costs.

Stock or order decisions depend on how generic and commonly used a part is; custom parts are definitely not stocked. Again, to maximize customer service, repair services must find vendors who can provide these parts in a timely manner.

Because the volume of repair work is somewhat unpredictable, capacity in terms of equipment and skilled employees is a major concern. Too few employees may generate substantial overtime; too many will cause idle time. Tracking productive time is essential. Often, a balance in capacity can be struck in part by having temporarily idle employees produce tooling. As long as it is necessary to the operation, charging the time as such is appropriate. One shudders to think, however, that tooling stocks will build up only never to find a use.

Compare that example with an electric motor repair shop that has a distribution operation. Capital requirements include storage facilities and material-handling equipment. Significant activities include sales, order picking, packaging, and shipping. The operation may include drop ship, in which the company's vendor ships directly to the customer. Generally, labor is less significant, as employees tend to be fewer in number and are on a lower pay scale.

In light of these disparate lines of business, financial reporting takes on a new significance. The traditional approach for departmental reporting, as mentioned earlier, is to match direct costs of each operation to its revenues in deriving its "contribution" to corporate selling and to general and administrative overhead. The approach is illustrated in Exhibit 6-1. Each contributes $2 million toward overhead of $3 million.

But as displayed in Exhibit 6-2, allocation of the overhead can affect perceptions significantly. If done on a sales basis, the distribution operation is clearly the loser; if done on a head-count basis, the repair operation loses. With such a significant figure in the balance, the issue deserves to be addressed.

The ABM approach is to assign those costs that are meaningful to assign. The operations have distinct sales forces that should be assigned. Operating managers, classified as corporate executive payroll, should likewise be assigned. You also need to analyze which operations truly utilize

Exhibit 6-1. Traditional Approach: Electric Motor Repair and Distribution Income Statement

DIVISIONAL INCOME STATEMENT
(*in thousands*)

	Repair	Distribution	Total
Sales	$6,000	$24,000	$30,000
Operating costs	(4,000)	(22,000)	(26,000)
Divisional contribution	$2,000	$ 2,000	$ 4,000
Corporate overhead			(3,000)
Net income			$ 1,000
Other data			
Divisional head count	60	15	

The traditional approach to product-line or divisional reporting is to assume that corporate selling, general, and administrative costs are "fixed," and that as long as a line or division makes a contribution to them, that line or division should remain open. The approach provides an answer to profitability that is often oversimplified.

Exhibit 6-2. Electric Motor Repair and Distribution Overhead Allocations

CORPORATE OVERHEAD ALLOCATIONS
(*in thousands*)

	Repair	Distribution	Total
Sales-based allocation:			
Divisional contribution	$2,000	$2,000	$4,000
Corporate overhead allocation (repair $6 mil., dist. $24 mil.)	600	2,400	3,000
Divisional net income (loss)	$1,400	$ (400)	$1,000
Head-count–based allocation:			
Divisional contribution	$2,000	$2,000	$4,000
Corporate overhead allocation (repair 60, dist. 15)	(2,400)	(600)	(3,000)
Divisional net income (loss)	$ (400)	$1,400	$1,000

As illustrated here, if corporate-level costs vary according to sales or to head count, the results for profitability are entirely different. Upon further analysis, it becomes apparent that certain operations require more support than others. Corporate-level costs should be assigned as appropriate.

the service departments. The repair operation is much more in need of payroll and personnel functions than the distribution one. Likewise, it is responsible for the job costing and order tracking systems. The distribution operation may consume more building maintenance because it occupies more square footage.

Insight into the specifics of these assignments, also known as "stage I" assignments, was covered in Chapter 3. Care should be taken, however, not to overdo them. Profitability of diverse product lines or decentralized operations must reflect only directly assignable costs. A budget must be constructed. Otherwise, the same mistake could be made in allocating general overhead as in allocating fixed costs in outsourcing decisions: Management could decide to discontinue a product line or close a facility based on losses that continue on.

Just as vital as distinguishing lines of business or product lines within your business is analysis by customer or distribution channel. As with products and services, customers differ in profitability. The key is having a reporting system detailed enough to account for the differences, so that meaningful information is available for decisions.

Awards Manufacturer

Let's turn to another case. A manufacturer of awards and specialty advertising items has a variety of distribution channels in place for which it has no means of assessing profitability. The channels include:

- *Trophy dealers.* Generally a small-order business, but requiring a minimum dollar size.
- *Distributors.* Allowed exclusive territorial rights to service trophy dealers within geographic limits.
- *National organizations and corporations.* Customers requiring custom items but in large quantities. The organizations' branches may order independently under a national contract, causing a large number of orders that otherwise would not meet preestablished minimums.

Without adequate costing, the company cannot address the following strategic issues:

- What are the savings incurred by selling through distributors as opposed to the overhead costs in selling direct?
- Are sales to national organizations still profitable after considering the effort involved?

Under ABM, these questions are answered through the development of models for applying sales, distribution, order, and lot-based costs. Just making such assignments may mean the difference between profit and loss, particularly for small orders.

Gaming Distributor

Finally, let's look at a gaming distributor that serves diverse national and local customers. Except in the case of certain volume discounts, the company charges both types of customers the same catalog prices.

Local accounts are independent retailers who directly cause certain costs. They require much sales support from the distributor in the form

Exhibit 6-3. ABM Approach: Gaming Distributor

PROFITABILITY BY CUSTOMER CATEGORY
(*in thousands*)

	National	Local	Total
Sales	$15,000	$15,000	$30,000
Cost of goods sold	(12,000)	(11,500)	(23,500)
Gross profit	$ 3,000	$ 3,500	$ 6,500
Operating costs	(1,000)	(4,000)	(5,000)
Operating profit (loss)	$ 2,000	$ (500)	$ 1,500
Other			500
Net income			$ 1,000

The classification of customers may make a significant difference in the level of un-charged services. Here, the lower margin achieved on national accounts is more than offset by additional operating expenses incurred by local ones.

of help with displays, suggestions for additional products, and even advice on running their businesses. Because their orders tend to be small, savings on freight-out are difficult to obtain. These customers also demand a wide variety of products, which means there must be a high level of inventory on hand. Some of these customers are start-ups and others are encountering financial problems, causing costs to carry and collect on the receivables.

The national accounts, on the other hand, are low credit risks, requiring minimal services. National accounts buy in large quantities, which reduces freight costs. They also frequently receive their orders by drop shipment, so that the distributor does not have to receive, stock, or ship the inventory.

With such a diverse range of services related to customer bases, the company needs to determine its profits by customer category. The results are shown in Exhibit 6-3. From this, the company can analyze the costs of the additional services and potential charges for them. Local accounts are not all losses. Some cause more costs than others. This calls for further distinction between the customers.

Practical Pointers

- The key to niche markets and competitive advantage is a thorough understanding of product and customer profitability. Traditional systems often take companies off-course. Redress of this problem calls for an objective reevaluation of what the true profits are.
- Viewing information in the new way under ABM leads to decisions that reduce areas of weakness and expand strengths.

Using ABM in insourcing and outsourcing decisions is covered next.

7

Insourcing and Outsourcing: Flagging Cost Leaks

Insourcing and outsourcing decisions are about whether to make or to buy. By their nature, these decisions—equally applicable to manufacturing and service companies—are part of a long-term strategy that determines a company's most significant commitment of resources. Almost every operation comes about because of these decisions, which involve choosing what type of specialization is most beneficial. Few entities make a finished product only from their own basic raw materials.

Considering the significance and complexity of such decisions, you'd hope that they would not be subject to the traditional "one size fits all" approach that is so overwhelmingly inadequate. But indeed they are. The result is bad information.

Insourcing and outsourcing merit only the most realistic accounting techniques. Here, ABM should be made a definite priority.

Outsourcing

You can be good at some things but admit that someone else is better at others. Outsourcing, the "buy" alternative, allows you to focus on what you're best at.

All new companies make outsourcing decisions, but they should know that conditions may change later. Existing companies make outsourcing decisions if they are expected to provide a package of products or services but can do only a part of the operation exceedingly well. Outsourcing may also occur temporarily if a company encounters an unexpected surge in demand in excess of present capacity, or when costly line changeover is the only alternative. Still other companies face outsourcing decisions daily when considering new orders.

Companies that strive to be a "jack of all trades" are "masters of none," as the old adage goes. Cost analysis is a continuous striving to understand your competitive advantage. If you employed two highly compensated specialists with experience on large projects, would you bid on a routine project? That would be a waste of their skills. It would be better to pass that type of work along to a company more suitably staffed for it.

Joint venturing involves a partner that complements a company's abilities. All costs considered, joint ventures may be the most cost-effective means of expanding your business. One company's niche capabilities may augment the strengths of others. Teaming up may provide a safe route for diversification into new areas, improve performance efficiency, expand market share, or simply increase financing capacity. Just being able to recognize the costs involved can help in making these decisions.

Unless the decisions are being made at the inception of the entity or of a new product, outsourcing decisions usually involve idling or disposing of major equipment. ABM is different from traditional methods in a major way in that it enables managers to account for this equipment and related costs.

Limits of Traditional Systems

Imagine a manager being offered an opportunity to outsource or enter a joint venture at a cost that sounds very reasonable. In attempting to assess the benefits, the manager contacts accounting to find out the costs of running the operation in-house. In response, accounting provides labor time and a **burden rate** (predetermined overhead rate). How much of that burden rate represents costs that would continue even after accepting the proposal? To answer that, accounting will need a few days to do projections—everybody's busy right now. Unless the proposal can wait, the opportunity may be lost.

The best traditional textbooks focus on **incremental** or **differential** costs of keeping the operation as opposed to farming it out. But these costs are not otherwise distinguished in cost accounting systems. It takes time to sort them out. The only information available immediately is labor time and a burden rate, or equivalent units and plant-costing rate.

As illustrated in Exhibit 7-1, the information at management's immediate disposal for evaluating make-or-buy alternatives may consist of simply comparing the costs of material, labor, and burden rate to the price quoted by the outside vendor. For process costing, departmental rates per equivalent unit of output are simply added together as costs to make the product. What is not evident is the true impact of the decision on costs.

A wrong reason for outsourcing is described in the following case study.

Exhibit 7-1. Traditional Approach: Make-or-Buy Decision

For 10,000 of Part X	Make	Buy
Material:		
Raw	$150,000	
Finished		$450,000
Labor:		
Two men (5,000 hrs. @ $10)	50,000	
Overhead:		
600% labor cost	300,000	
Total	$500,000	$450,000
Profit from outsourcing	$ 50,000	

This is the type of information readily available from traditional systems. The oversimplification of costs can be highly misleading.

MACHINERY-MAKER CORP.

After years of lackluster performance, the management of Machinery-Maker Corp. determines from its cost information that it would be cheaper to outsource certain major operations. After months of outsourcing result in more losses than ever in the company's history, the controller's information is questioned. "I calculated our hourly rates the way we always have," he laments. "By total manufacturing overhead divided by direct labor hours charged. I can't explain these results." The company turns to ABM.

Results: The ABM analysis reveals that costs are being misapplied. A company engaging in mass outsourcing should not apply unrelated operation costs to shrinking labor hours. To do so is a classic example of overapplication. The company should exclude costs relating to the handling of purchased items, idled manufacturing capacity, fixed occupancy, and other costs from its hourly rates. Otherwise, work will continue to be farmed out, rates will continue to increase, and even more work will be farmed out so that vendor prices for outsourcing will appear to be more and more attractive. With the same sales volume and a decreased distributor's margin, along with overheads from its new methods, idled manufacturing capacity, and fixed costs, the company may find itself hard pressed. The company will end up without manufacturing operations, and ultimately, without a business.

Even in less drastic situations, traditional costing has lingering deleterious effects. In systems that undercost complex, custom, or other nonroutine work, and correspondingly overcost simpler operations, the long-term implication is that the simpler ones will be outsourced or lost to competitors. The underpriced complex items will increase in share of the product mix and, without the hidden profits of simpler operations for support, margins will deteriorate. Costs will suddenly appear excessive in relation to volume. Oversimplicity strikes again! Correcting the cost system is the first step in saving the business. Complex decisions merit a detailed technique for analysis.

Outsourcing under ABM

Instead of engaging in abstract terminology, ABM uses the "activities" that the traditional cost system has already defined. The question now becomes, "Which activities will cease or continue under outsourcing as compared with going ahead as is?" The answer is immediately available.

With ABM budgets, cost records may be ignored in the make-or-buy decision. As a practical matter, only those activities that discontinue under outsourcing should be used in determining the cost to make. If the company already owns the equipment, equipment depreciation, occupancy, and other costs fixed in the near term are irrelevant to the decision. The proper ABM approach is presented in Exhibit 7-2.

Some activities and their associated costs continue. "Variable" activities like material handling and inspection must occur whether the parts arrive raw or finished. Depreciation appears under both alternatives because it is a noncash expense representing allocation of an asset's historical cost, which will not be saved through outsourcing. ABM allows you to understand the operations well enough to get back to the true "incremental" costs of the decision in a way everyone understands.

Insourcing

Insourcing means bringing in-house an operation that has previously been performed by a supplier or customer. It is the "make" alternative in a make-or-buy decision. As such, it usually involves acquisition of new equipment and people.

The benefits of insourcing and other capital expenditures are at the

Exhibit 7-2. ABM Approach: Make-or-Buy Decision

	Make	Buy
Purchased material:		
Raw	$150,000	
Finished		$450,000
Process costs:		
Maintenance	10,000	
Operators	50,000	
Operator taxes and benefits	10,000	
Power	10,000	
Supplies	5,000	
Tooling	5,000	
Support costs:		
Accounting	10,000	5,000
Administrative	15,000	5,000
Inspection	15,000	10,000
Material handling	20,000	10,000
Supervision	10,000	5,000
Related taxes and benefits	15,000	10,000
Fixed costs:		
Equipment depreciation	75,000	75,000
Occupancy	90,000	90,000
Executive compensation	10,000	10,000
Total	$500,000	$670,000
Loss from outsourcing	$170,000	

With ABM, you can readily adapt activity analysis to make-or-buy decisions. With outsourcing, certain activities will discontinue, whereas others will continue at potentially differing rates.

heart of a new operation and create potential competitive advantages. The right investment can prove the difference between a company's life and death. But the decision should consider effects on the operation as a whole.

Because of the huge costs, acquiring equipment means the commitment of long-term resources, so your objectives must be clearly specified and understood. For example, you may want to update technology or begin a new product line, or another piece of equipment may enable your company to avoid costly setup or changeover by allowing for dedication to a certain type of product or operation.

If the purpose of the expenditure is to improve productivity, will the benefits outweigh the costs? If the purpose is to increase capacity or enter a new market, will the demand be there? Too often, companies acquire high-capacity machinery for insourcing, assuming that they can sell any excess capacity in the marketplace. When the external demand fails to materialize, they are stuck with debt obligations and overhead costs incurred by an underutilized machine.

Sometimes, the effects of insourcing and capacity expansion beyond market utilization can depress entire industries. Commercial real estate in the 1980s, initially spurred by temporary tax incentives, is a prime example—in this case, of an excessive increase in facilities. Another is the paper industry, where boom-and-bust cycles result from overly optimistic capacity planning. In commodity industries, pursuing economies of scale without adequately considering market constraints can adversely affect even the higher-margin custom-finishing industries (such as box shops) as paper converters attempt to vertically integrate to capture profits.

Moreover, if the proposed equipment is not in sync with present equipment and configuration, productivity may not increase. Managers may wonder why an expensive new machine has no effect on total output. Work-in-process stacked at the next operation may be the answer: Bottlenecks have formed, preventing efficiency gains from being realized; at the low utilization level caused by constraints, the new machine may have been a mistake.

Motivations that can destroy a company include empire-building or excessive company pride. Manufacturing managers insist that bringing operations in-house preserves confidentiality, increases quality, and heightens control over timing. If pursued for only these reasons, the result is disaster in the form of lack of know-how relative to the new business line. With everything in-house and operating losses higher than ever, managers have only themselves to blame. They must accept the fact that no company can be best at everything and search for what the company *is* good at. As incidentals are outsourced, renewed profitability can result.

Even traditional cost systems may motivate insourcing or automation for the wrong reasons, as discussed in the following case.

ELECTRONIC COMPONENTS CO.

Electronic Components Co. is considering its fourth purchase of "labor-saving" equipment this year. "With an overhead rate of 400 percent," argues a department manager, "reducing labor by $10,000 will save us $40,000 in overhead—more than enough to pay for the equipment." Somehow, the savings are never realized. Because costs continue to increase, management decides to try ABM to find out why.

Results: ABM analysis determines that the problem is in the company's cost system.

When departmentalized companies use a single job-costing burden rate, overhead becomes a hot potato. New equipment seems to lower the acquiring department's costs significantly, because the cost is spread over the entire plant. So department managers are motivated to automate as much as possible. But is what's best for the department also best for the plant? Definitely not. The new equipment costs mean that savings are never fully realized. Expenditures to automate operations clearly cause higher overhead in the form of depreciation, energy, maintenance, and indirect labor costs. The shifting of overhead from departmentwide to plantwide obscures losses incurred, inhibiting a weighing of benefits and costs. Once ABM is implemented, the problem stops, because the counterproductive motivation is removed.

Capital Budgeting Techniques

Like budgets, planned capital expenditures should be linked to the strategic plan. Policies should specify the manner of formal authorization. For information to support the decisions, traditional textbooks discuss **capital budgeting models.**

In deciding between long-term alternatives, traditional capital budgeting models are set up to provide uniform yardsticks by which to judge investments in two ways:

1. *Payback.* This measures the number of years required to recover the initial investment outlay.
2. *Discounted cash flow.* Whether the statistic of interest is rate of re-

turn or present value, its calculation entails scheduling of cash flows discounted at an assumed rate.

While these two models provide guidelines, no model, regardless of its sophistication, can support a decision without reasonable evidence of the following:

* Proper measurement of costs and benefits, which, as we have seen, traditional costing does not provide
* Options regarding the extent of utilization

How you can address these concerns practically is the subject of the following sections.

Insourcing and ABM

Proper measurement of costs primarily involves analyses along the lines of Exhibit 7-2. Activities attributable to insourcing or capital expenditures must be fully contemplated and accounted for. Elements peculiar to insourcing decisions include learning, measuring the investment, and assessing the fit with operations.

Whenever you introduce a new operation, you can expect certain costs. Capital expenditure decisions, because they involve people, require learning, such as training and practice runs. Industrial engineers construct standard learning curves to reflect this, but actual past experience is probably just as accurate.

To decide whether to insource, you must identify the direct costs of the investment. Exclude depreciation, because it does not represent an outflow of cash. Include debt obligations, financing costs, and incremental overhead.

Finally, the fit of the equipment with existing operations is important. Promised benefits will not materialize where bottlenecks in other operations develop.

Breakeven Utilization

The most difficult yet important factor to predict when making an insourcing decision is how you will use the new resource. Because you can only estimate this, you should develop a range with which to assess potential benefits. A **breakeven utilization model** provides the limits of this range.

Breakeven utilization is determined in the same way as other breakeven models: You compare fixed outflows, like financing payments and equipment overhead, with the expected margin per unit of activity. This approach is shown in Exhibit 7-3.

Note that the annual breakeven utilization in Exhibit 7-3 is 2,000 units. The result could just as easily have been stated in hours of output, operations performed, or whatever cost driver measure is most appropriate for reflecting the underlying activity.

Practical Guidelines for Insourcing Decisions

To summarize, costs associated with a new operation include the initial investment, fixed overhead, and variable (volume-related) costs. The ABM approach is a line-by-line before-and-after listing of costs, as shown in Exhibit 7-4. Determining the appropriate projected amounts that will be incurred "after" bringing the operation in-house requires relating costs to

Exhibit 7-3. Breakeven Utilization

Sales contribution per unit	$ 80
Less direct costs per unit	
Procurement	(5)
Process	(20)
Delivery	(5)
Profit per unit, before investment costs	$ 50
Annual investment costs	
Debt obligations or depreciation	$ 50,000
Occupancy	25,000
Other	25,000
Total	$100,000
Breakeven annual utilization	
Annual investment costs	$100,000
Profit per unit	$50
Annual utilization in units	2,000

In deciding whether or not to acquire new machinery or operations, the extent of utilization is an essential but uncertain element. Analysis of breakeven utilization provides a range of comfort or discomfort.

Exhibit 7-4. Make-or-Buy Decision: Format

	Buy (Before)	Make (After)
Initial investment		
Equipment costs	n/a	$_____
Tooling purchases	n/a	_____
Setup costs	n/a	_____
Learning costs	n/a	_____
Total		$_____
Fixed overhead		
Occupancy	$_____	$_____
Indirect labor	_____	_____
Other	_____	_____
Total	$_____	$_____
Variable costs		
Direct material	$_____	$_____
Material-related costs	_____	_____
Direct labor	_____	_____
Labor-related costs	_____	_____
Normal inefficiency	_____	_____
Variable indirect labor	_____	_____
Equipment-related costs	_____	_____
Other operating costs	_____	_____
Total	$_____	$_____

The form covers the three cost categories of concern when making insourcing decisions: initial investment, fixed overhead, and variable costs.

their causes. This is where ABM activity drivers come in. You may estimate the change in certain maintenance costs, for example, by using the anticipated increase in machine hours, and the change in certain purchasing costs by using the increase in purchase orders, and so on.

An explanation of the three categories of costs follows.

1. *Initial investment.* The initial investment category includes the one-time outlays associated with bringing in manufacturing. Examples are

equipment costs, additional tooling purchases, initial setup, and learning costs. **Learning costs** include training and practice runs, which you may either estimate or determine by using a standard engineering formula. The total resulting from the combination of these elements represents the investment that savings from bringing the operation in-house must recover.

2. *Fixed overhead.* Costs defined as "fixed" for purposes of the insourcing decision are those unaffected by the activity level of the proposed operation. This category includes additional occupancy and certain indirect labor costs associated with the new operation. Occupancy consists of such items as rent, depreciation, utilities, real estate taxes, security, maintenance, and insurance. Indirect labor includes supervision, administration, purchasing, or other payroll costs that will not change with activity levels. Related payroll costs should be added, such as payroll taxes, insurance, and other benefits. Where applicable, you should also include other related costs such as supplies.

3. *Variable costs.* Variable or "nonfixed" costs relate to the *level* of activities. Analyze the following categories:

- *Direct material.* The costs of "before" and "after" should reflect the savings that result from buying raw products for in-house processing. Direct material costs should include freight-in and discounts.
- *Material-related costs.* These costs include those associated with carrying inventory, such as property insurance, indirect labor, and related equipment costs.
- *Direct labor.* This category includes base pay of the additional direct labor required for insourcing.
- *Labor-related costs.* Related costs cover payroll taxes, insurance, union dues, pensions, and other benefits.
- *Normal inefficiency.* Because no operation can run at 100 percent efficiency all of the time, you need to include downtime, rework, and scrap costs.
- *Variable indirect labor.* Indirect labor consists of such activities as scheduling, production control, and inspection, plus related benefits.
- *Equipment-related costs.* These include maintenance, supplies, energy, and related indirect labor.
- *Other operating costs.* Miscellaneous items include outside services, supplies, tools, dies, spare parts, and indirect materials.

Once it is completed, you can use the results of the analysis for the following:

- *Payback period.* The net savings in fixed overhead and variable costs per period (month, year) can be divided into the initial investment to obtain a payback period, which represents the number of periods that will occur before you recover the investment.
- *Breakeven utilization.* If the net savings in variable costs are translated to a per-unit or driver basis, the initial investment plus the increase in fixed overhead costs can be divided by the per-unit savings to derive breakeven production per period.

These calculations should help you to determine whether bringing the operation in-house will increase profits.

Lease-or-Buy Analysis

Once you have decided to insource a given operation, your next decision may be whether to lease or buy the new equipment. The determination is completely mechanical up to a point: Just compare the present value of the lease payments with the costs of ownership. Include the purchase cost of the equipment plus the present value of maintenance or other lessor services minus the equipment's residual value.

In the course of your analysis, you'll find that whether you lease or buy will depend on how long you plan to use the equipment. If it's forever, it's usually best to purchase, whereas if it's for three years, you'll probably do better to lease.

One variable that the mechanical calculations cannot reflect is obsolescence. When you buy, you commit yourself to present technology. Think of how personal computers progressed from the late 1980s to the mid-1990s! Distributed data processing has now replaced mainframe systems with PC networks. Who knows what the next five years will bring?

Other Investments

American management has been criticized for being shortsighted and un-innovative and as having a tendency to favor "quick fixes." If this is true, one reason may be our traditional financial accounting methods, which do not recognize investments in the intangible areas that affect a company's future. Although these intangible costs, e.g., those for long-sighted projects such as research, system improvements, training, and preventive maintenance, are as essential to a company's future as machinery and equipment, they are written off as current expenses. While recognizing these costs as assets is not necessarily desirable, they are definitely distinct in nature and should be visibly separated in reporting.

Practical Pointers

- To ensure integrity of information, analysis of costs should always draw upon ABM data. Because ABM is so comprehensive, the data are immediately available to support analysis of a wide variety of decisions.
- Insourcing and outsourcing decisions rely on the availability of detailed cost information for every product or service. The details are usually in cost-estimating formats, the subject of the next chapter.
- Breakeven analyses have wide application, and are illustrated in detail in Chapter 11.

8

Improving Bidding,
Estimating, and Pricing
with ABM

In the past, estimating was considered to be a highly specialized function calling for in-depth knowledge of products or services. An estimator's judgment was based on a set of unwritten rules learned from experience—rules passed along from generation to generation but seldom documented, and rarely tested formally on an ongoing basis. Under these circumstances, it was difficult to replace estimators who retired or otherwise created a vacancy.

Traditional systems still generally use a job-cost approach that accounts for only a small portion of the costs of doing business. The rest is "fudged" through percentage markups for overhead and profit. Process cost systems are even less detailed because they do not track so-called direct costs. Obviously, such bidding procedures should be reconsidered.

As with any other business activity, ABM implementation improves bidding, estimating, and pricing as a matter of course. From an estimating standpoint, ABM's objective is to make the relationships between costs and the peculiar characteristics that estimators look for both evident and testable. These peculiar characteristics take the form of activity drivers, which are documented in estimating product costs and tested through budgeting.

Estimating and Bidding

A major value of documenting estimates and integrating them into the reporting system is that it eliminates conflicts between sales and manufacturing. The sales department is motivated to give the customer all the

variety desired, whereas manufacturing is concerned with attaining efficiencies through long production runs of limited-variety items. What sales
promises may not be what manufacturing can deliver.

Documentation ensures that there is one true explanation to which
both sales and manufacturing are accountable. The costs of extravagance
are now appropriately reflected, and manufacturing is expected to live up
to estimates. An ideal system would provide incentives toward a coopera-
tive meeting of expectations.

Traditional Approach

Recall Exhibit 7-1. Its format could just as easily reflect the traditional
approach used in estimating: material plus labor marked up for overhead.
The job-cost pattern shown treats labor and material as the only factors
worth considering. Say an estimator using the form must quote on an
order that will run across a new machine that, once set up, runs unattended. (Today, unlike the days in which these cost systems were designed, machines run practically unattended, and direct laborers are
outnumbered by indirect and administrative personnel.) Should the estimator fill in only the setup, which on a large run is only a fraction of total
time? Or, in the absence of traditional "direct" labor, is the cost actually
zero? As an interim response, the estimator may use machine time, but
ultimately he or she must take an activity-driver approach.

Nowadays, most overhead relates to characteristics of orders other
than their labor content. The relationship between costs such as those for
automation, plant administration, occupancy, material-related cost, and
inefficiency is tenuous at best. So too with process costing. The diversity
of costs precludes all of them from being related to a single **equivalent
unit.** Building costs, inefficiencies, plant management, payroll-related
costs, and automation unrelated to product weight bear little relation to a
tons base, for example.

The failure of traditional estimating is clear. To cushion product costs,
which continue to behave less and less like the traditional models, fudge
factors for markup increase. Otherwise, bad bids would quickly turn into
losses. But since the fudge factors have no relationship to actual costs and
profits, companies are being fooled into thinking their estimating system
is adequate.

The examples up until now have dealt with companies using job-cost
systems, in which direct material and labor are charged by order. Repetitive manufacturers using process cost approaches face similar problems.
These systems take total production costs and divide them over an equiv-

alent unit. But how do you define the most suitable equivalent unit? The difficulty in answering that question is that most companies are too complex for a single base to be effective. Consider the following case.

SCRAP ALUMINUM PROCESSOR CO.

Scrap Aluminum Processor Co. uses weight as a basis for purchasing raw scrap and selling finished coil. Naturally, it follows that weight in pounds commonly functions as the industry's "equivalent unit" for applying costs. The pounds base is divided into budgeted departmental or plantwide manufacturing costs to derive a cost per pound. For example, $50 million in costs divided by 100 million pounds comes out to 50 cents per pound. So the cost of a finished coil weighing 10,000 pounds after going through all operations is calculated as costing $5,000. Moreover, process costing simply averages in downtime or any other inefficiency. Management, suspecting that this system is not providing adequate information, switches to ABM.

Results: ABM reveals the system's inadequacies by looking into operations: melting, casting, hot rolling, cold rolling, annealing, slitting, and leveling. Because melting, casting, and hot rolling use molten material, the end product is uniform. Their costs can be based on pounds but could just as well be based on cost per coil, lineal foot, or some other measure. It is in the finishing costs— cold rolling, annealing, slitting, and leveling—that significant distortions occur. Cold rolling reduces the gauge or thickness of the material. Depending on customer specifications, a coil may be cold-rolled once, twice, or even six times. Using pounds as the basis for costs allocates the costs equally to coils of the same weight regardless of the number of passes through rolling. The *number of times* rolled would appear to be a more appropriate basis for applying costs.

Similarly, the annealing process, which softens metal by baking, is heavily dependent on customer tension tolerances. The particular heat level and baking time heavily influence costs and provide a better basis than pounds. Slitting and leveling operations depend on machinery with run speeds stated in feet per minute. Here, the length of the material determines run cost incurred. This, then, would be preferable to using pounds, particularly because of the substantial footage variance resulting from rolling.

ABM Approach

Most essential to providing a reasonable basis for estimating is the resource usage path (see Chapters 2 and 3).

The understanding can go beyond the bidding function to what composes financial results. You can use the same drivers identified for bidding in budgeting operations, as described in Chapter 2. The up-to-date information for product costing monitors efficiencies in all areas of your organization.

Estimating forms should reflect actual cost behavior. Instead of extending labor time, units, or markup percentages, the factors used should include the cost drivers consumed by the activities associated with the order. The key to being able to bid and predict profitability is understanding the costs provided by ABM.

The document linking the budgeting and estimating systems is the **bill of activities.** It is similar to a bill of materials, but substitutes for materials a list of the activities that are performed from acceptance of the order to shipment and collection. More than a routing, it lists the quantity of activity drivers for the product and the budgeted costing rate per unit of activity driver, tested through comparison to actual costs through budgeting.

Note that this crucial document uses terms understood by everyone familiar with the operation, not just by estimators. Characteristics of measurements, such as weight, footage, and pieces, are easily communicated, even across departments. The process of estimating costs now means measuring these characteristics or activity drivers. The amount consumed by the activities necessary to produce the product is extended at the budgeted rates to determine cost.

A typical estimating form sequence may be described for a manufacturer as follows:

- Material, purchasing, handling, and other related costs, including charges for scrap generated by the order
- Process costs, reflecting appropriate drivers for each operation
- Packaging and shipping costs, driven by appropriate order characteristics
- Selling costs, particularly sales commissions
- Administrative costs, including order processing

See the specific examples discussed at the end of this chapter. You should provide for detailed as well as budget-level comparison of estimated and actual costs. If the variances are out of line, investigate them further.

Pricing

Pricing decisions depend on a multitude of factors. Two of the largest determinants are market and cost. The degree of their relative significance may vary substantially by industry.

Market-Based Pricing

Unless a company has a monopoly, pricing is affected by the marketplace. Because customers who obtain multiple quotes are aware of what competitors charge, outrageous pricing policies, like $100 per cup of lemonade, attract no business.

Companies with highly competitive markets, like commodities, must accept the market price, but they should assess the contribution to profit made by each of their products, with a view toward determining which ones to emphasize.

Cost-Based Pricing

Pricing based on cost requires setting markups, which can take the form of multipliers representing the inverse of expected gross profit. To obtain a gross profit of 40 percent after product costs, you can use a multiplier of 1.67 $[1/(1 - .4)]$ as a normal markup.

An example of cost-driven pricing is the billing by professional firms—law, engineering, or accounting. Here, employees log actual time spent by project for extension at a rate intended to capture costs plus budgeted profit. Again, however, time or rates that are outside of what's reasonable for the market will cause customers to go elsewhere.

Variations between Market- and Cost-Based Pricing

The variations between market sensitivity and cost factors in pricing are infinite. Whether prices are set in a catalog or based on customer specification, the customer is usually unaware of how much they are actually driven by costs as opposed to market factors allowing for high or low markups.

With certain services, like auto repair, customers may desire fixed-fee quotes; nonetheless, cost estimating plays a significant role. Under fixed-fee systems, the company bears the risk of unforeseen difficulties with the job, which may cause additional time. As a result, simpler jobs must be overcharged to compensate for the complicated ones, so the customer with the routine job ends up paying more. To remain competitive and reduce their own risk, auto repair services should identify characteristics known to cause higher costs up front before accepting work at the fixed rate. That way, they can negotiate a charge for the extra work that actually causes the costs.

How can you use pricing to remove subsidies that may occur in your operation? That is the subject of the next case.

LOAN UNDERWRITING CO.

Loan Underwriting Co. underwrites loan applications provided by brokers and other customers. Competing services are beginning to encroach upon its market. Management decides to find out why costs are so high internally and discovers that the time to process the loans varies widely depending on the quality of the information submitted. Upon further investigation, it appears that a few customers are responsible for most of the additional costs. While on average the operations are profitable, the practice of fixed-fee quotes hides the actual state of affairs, in which losses generated by these few customers are offset or subsidized by the other customers. The company applies ABM.

Results: The ABM study finds that roughly half the total costs are spent performing additional activities caused by the failure of certain customers to submit proper applications. To counter the problem, the company decides to charge these customers back. It implements the following procedures:

- ◆ Prices are reduced overall for applications submitted without problems. This immediately counters the encroachment of other services.
- ◆ A chargeback policy is established for applications requiring additional work. An allowance of five corrections per month is given each customer, beyond which the customer is charged an additional processing fee.
- ◆ The problem customers are forewarned about the new policy. This includes sending pseudo-billings so that these customers know what to expect.
- ◆ Problem customers also receive manuals specifying how to comply with submission requirements.

While some of the problem customers are lost, those that remain begin to clean up their submissions. Profitable business grows as new customers turn to the company for its lower prices. Sales volume and margin increase.

Fixed and Variable Costs

Some accountants recommend the use of **incremental, differential,** or **variable** costs in pricing, similar to what's used for outsourcing decisions.

A company engaging in one or all of these strategies may initially obtain business, but it will shortly find that in retaliation, its competitors may assail its customer base in the same way it has assailed theirs. Even if the sales level is the same when the dust clears, the profit margins will suffer. Lower variable contribution means that fixed costs will not be covered. The company must then try to recover its lost profitable accounts. But, as anyone with marketing or sales experience will tell you, cutting prices to the variable-contribution or incremental-cost bone can ruin a market, which will then take years to rebuild. Price cutting does not build stable, profitable industries. The recent downfall of so many discount appliance dealers bears out this observation.

At best, these techniques are useful for incremental orders; under-pricing should never be used as a long-term pricing strategy. Over the long term, all that is fixed becomes variable, and unless fixed costs have been covered in pricing, the company will lose money. The costs include many that are relevant to products, such as supervision and depreciation.

Moreover, variable-contribution pricing does not make sense when a manual operation is supplemented with an automated one. In an entirely manual operation, costs directly associated with the product are mostly variable, but as companies automate, a larger portion of total costs becomes fixed, e.g., depreciation, debt obligations, and insurance associated with the machine. Because variable costs per unit of output decrease, pricing on that basis will cause an excessive load on the automated operation relative to the high-cost manual one, without providing for recovery of the investment. As is again apparent from the example, general pricing policies, other than in certain exceptional situations, should assume full costs.

This does not mean that if you incur $1 million in starting an operation and produce only one good unit, these costs should be recaptured in pricing. As was covered in more detail in Chapter 3, costs that are fixed, such as equipment depreciation or occupancy costs, may require distinct treatment to reflect normal volume. The analysis should lead to an understanding of profits and pricing for a proper margin.

Toward a Pricing Strategy

Essential to a pricing strategy is a **normal profit idea,** or the amount that goods or services are expected to contribute on average, to be determined through formal budgeting. Through awareness of markets, managers can make decisions to **value bill** (billing customers according to a *perception* of value rather than according to standard rates) or achieve excess profit on certain niche items, or they may accept lower profits when trying to break into a new market. Markup decisions may be correlated with capacity availability.

Perhaps for the first time, you will have true cost and profit information to enable you to adjust sales commission systems or determine areas of emphasis and competitive advantage. Note that cost should always be an objective and visible barometer. Managers who understate estimated costs to make certain orders from favored customers appear profitable are simply kidding themselves.

Minimum-Order and Volume Discounts

Once the lot-based activities introduced in Chapter 3 have been fully identified and costed, they may serve as bases for determining minimum-order and volume discounts. You will recall that lot-based costs, e.g., order costs and setup, are incurred by groups or lots of units, not by unit. If you so choose, you can develop additional charges to cover these costs using normal profit margins.

Examples

General Contractor Example

Exhibit 8-1 lists the significant activities performed by general contractors, which were covered in more detail in Chapter 4. Clearly, only a small portion of their costs relate to the traditional direct-labor or volume bases.

As shown in Exhibits 8-2 and 8-3, there is no change of directly charged costs of material, contractors, and labor from traditional approaches. Overhead, however, makes a significant difference in profitability, which traditional methods ignore. The traditional method does not recognize costs of managing subcontractors, administering sites, purchasing, or catering to special needs that are presumably allocated on the basis of the estimators' judgment. Improving estimating to reflect these factors can make a big difference. The ABM approach shows that the small order generates a substantial loss, compared to what appears to be normal profit using the traditional approach.

Additional Examples

Remember the steel service company and the delivery service operations discussed in Chapter 4? Estimating forms suitable to each operation are described in turn.

Exhibit 8-1. Activities Performed by General Contractors

- Bidding and engineering, including request for quotations on material prices or work contracted out
- Procurement of material, equipment, and contractors' services
- Maintenance of material stocks and owned equipment
- Project management and administration, including oversight of other contractors
- Performance of certain work, e.g., carpentry
- Corporate-level management and administration
- Maintenance of information systems sufficient to provide reporting to the general contractor's management, project owners, and other external users

Activities performed by general contractors are diverse. Very few relate to labor or equivalent units in a realistic way.

Exhibit 8-2. Traditional Approach: Sample General Contractor's Estimating Form

Description	Rate	Usage	Project A	Project B
Contract price			$50,000	$500,000
Costs:				
Material	$100/unit	100	$10,000	
		1,000		$100,000
Subcontractors	$75/unit	100	7,500	
		1,000		75,000
Direct labor	$10/hr.	500	5,000	
		5,000		50,000
Overhead	300% labor hrs.	N/A	15,000	
		N/A		150,000
Total			$37,500	$375,000
Gross profit			$12,500	$125,000
Gross profit percentage			25%	25%

The traditional general contractor's estimating form includes direct charges for material, subcontractors, and direct labor. Remaining costs are allocated across labor. This method ignores the analysis of activities presented in Exhibit 7-1.

Exhibit 8-3. ABM Approach: Sample General Contractor's Estimating Form

Description	Rate	Usage	Project A	Project B
Contract price			$50,000	$500,000
Costs:				
Material	$100/unit	100	10,000	
		1,000		100,000
Contractors	$75/unit	100		7,500
		1,000		75,000
Labor	$10/hour	500	5,000	
		5,000		50,000
Purchasing	$50/po	200	10,000	
		350		17,500
Project costs	$5,000/proj.	1	5,000	5,000
		5	12,500	
Project admin.	$2,500/contractor	8		20,000
Special requirements			5,000	7,500
Other overhead charged by causal relationship			5,000	45,000
Total			$60,000	$320,000
Gross profit (loss)			$(10,000)	$180,000
Gross profit (loss) percentage			(20%)	36%

The ABM approach to estimating, in contrast to the traditional approach, is based on analysis of significant activities and how these affect costs. The more realistic model can turn profitability perceptions around. Certain projects are not worth the effort entailed.

Steel Service Operation The steel service operation purchases coils of steel approximately 36 inches wide and slits them to customer-specified widths. A purchased master coil may be slit into several narrower finished coils. Significant issues in the operation include scrap, treatment of off-fall material, and lot-based costs such as setup and special customer services.

A traditional cost system for a steel service operation very much resembles the contractor's estimating form shown in Exhibit 8-2. Direct material and labor are charged to production runs, with overhead added as a factor of labor. There is little insight into the actual causes of overhead for purposes of order costing and control.

See what happens when the steel service operation implements the ABM approach to estimating, as presented in Exhibit 8-4. Here, cost assignment for estimating purposes reflects underlying operations. The

Exhibit 8-4. ABM Approach: Sample Steel Service Estimating Form

Description	Rate	Usage	Extension
Material and coil costs:			
Raw material	$.20/lb.	25,000 lbs.	$5,000
Material handling	$50/coil	2	100
Setup	$65/setup	1	65
Subtotal		25,000 lbs.	$5,165
Yield loss	4%	1,000	
Scrap recovery	$.05/lb.	1,000	(50)
Subtotal, all orders		24,000 lbs.	$5,115
Less material required	order	17,000 lbs.	
Leftover material		7,000	
Apply to other orders		5,000	
Chargeable leftover	$20/lb.	2,000	400
Less scrap recovery	$.05/lb.	2,000	(100)
Subtotal, this order form		17,000 lbs.	$5,415
Processing and other services:			
Slitting, medium gauge	$.10/ft.	2,400 ft.	240
Less portion charged to other orders			($50)
Order activities	$50/order	1	50
Shipping		$20/pallet	220
Special requirements			0
Risks: rework, downtime	.01/ft.	2,400 ft.	24
TOTAL	.335/lb.	17,000 lbs.	$5,899

As is the case with Exhibit 8-3, the approach to estimating presented here relates closely to underlying operations. This is a differentiating characteristic of ABM.

form is separated into (1) material and coil costs and (2) processing and other services. Material-handling and setup costs are assigned to raw material on a per-coil basis. The costs of scrap and leftover-material-less-scrap-recoveries are then determined.

On the second half of the form, only that portion of the coil applied to the particular order being estimated is carried forward. Slitting is assigned on a per-foot basis, less the portion charged to other orders. Order and shipping costs are added next, followed by special services as applicable. Finally, the company may choose to apply an optional risk factor representing discretionary downtime and rework costs.

The result should represent the costs associated with the order as realistically as possible. Setup, material-handling, and slitting costs are akin to fixed costs when potential additional orders for the given coil are being considered. The efficiency of coil utilization may correspondingly affect pricing of the order—issues not addressed by traditional job-cost systems.

Delivery Service Operation   Delivery services, while entirely different from steel services, share many of the same costing problems. The profitability of a given route is determined by the number of stops and their pricing. Like lot- or coil-based costs, costs associated with routes are fixed with respect to accepting an additional stop.

The first section of the form shown in Exhibit 8-5 shows that delivery

---

Exhibit 8-5. ABM Approach: Sample Delivery Service Estimating Form

Description	Rate	Usage	Extension
Route costs:			
In-transit	.60/min.	300	$180
	.40/mi.	50	20
Other route costs	150/route	1	150
Total route costs			$350
Less portion to other stops			(335)
Total, these stops			$15
Direct costs:			
Pickup	.30/min.	5	2
	.20/mi.	3	1
Delivery	.30/min.	3	1
	.20/mi.	8	2
Contract processing	1/order	1	1
All requirements:			0
TOTAL COST			$ 22

As in the preceding exhibit for steel service, the form is divided between lot- or otherwise nonorder-level costs, and direct costs of accepting the order. This is intended to reflect the significant operational issues of the business.

service estimating begins with route costs, including time in transit, mileage between the route and the base, and other costs such as depreciation, licensing, insurance, and maintenance. The costs are applied to the pickup and delivery stops in question by excluding those relating to other stops.

The second section of the form represents direct costs of the stop in question. Time is based on how much is spent at each stop. Mileage is determined as half the distance between the previous and next stops, or simply the previous or next stop if it is the first or last stop on the route. For customers requiring same-day pickup and delivery, the entire distance between pickup and delivery points might be included in the estimate.

Finally, the form contains order and special customer requirement costs. Management can use the resulting total cost in determining the contribution for the stops in question. Management expects new routes to lose money until utilization is increased sufficiently to break even.

With ABM, estimating can evolve into a process that for the first time is verifiable and relates to actual operations. While no form can supplant judgment entirely, significant factors may be formularized for everyone's understanding.

Practical Pointers

- ◆ Estimating formats should contain all necessary information for making the calculations mechanical and reviewable. Only in this manner is it possible to ensure accuracy through the flexible budgeting tie-in to actual financial results.
- ◆ Special requirements activities discovered in ABM analysis may lead to changes in profitability assessments and even have ramifications for pricing.
- ◆ To have the most impact, profitability and costing should also affect employee evaluation and compensation, the subject of the next chapter.

9

Incentive Compensation:
The Importance of Accuracy

Once you understand costs, you can introduce new ways of motivating people—and even encourage them to work together. If you've truly clarified your company's goals, it's easy to get people to meet them. Unfortunately, like every other aspect of business, incentive systems suffer from inadequate data and an oversimplified definition of productivity or output; managers have no idea what their incentive systems are costing them.

Existing incentive systems have many shortfalls. Although they have been part of business since the Industrial Revolution, they are still structured according to the same one-size-fits-all mentality used by traditional cost systems. But by making the causes of costs visible, you can create an incentive system that will direct individuals to avoid those costs and reduce their effects.

Inadequacies of Traditional Incentive Systems

Typically, compensation is in the form of bonuses or pay per piece, and the common objective is to vary compensation according to relative productivity. But do you really know how productive your workers are? Traditional incentive systems are likely to have several effects.

Pure Waste

Waste occurs if the work being measured is difficult to verify after its completion.

HOMEBUILDER CO.

In areas like drywall or wiring, using a piece or productivity incentive to compensate the crew requires a way of measuring output. If the material is installed at the job site, the amount can only be derived from what was taken to the site and not returned. When managers discover that this system encourages the crew to discard any materials in excess of their needs, the managers are at first astonished and then undertake to investigate why.

Results: They discover that employees are reacting to the indirect motivations built in to the system. When the the system is changed, the waste goes away.

Poor Quality

Inadequate quality control systems can breed disastrous results. For example, crediting labor for number of pieces produced may encourage production of low-quality or defective items. As long as work is inspected after the completion of production and the involvement of several departments, it will be impossible to trace who exactly is responsible for defects. So all the workers get the incentive pay regardless.

Unless the costs of poor quality are made visible by the system, managers will be unaware of what their incentives are doing. No amount of lecturing about total quality management will remove the motivation for such behavior. It will continue until systematically removed or redirected toward rewards for quality.

Cherry Picking

Output may be measured in terms of equal units of production, but the actual work required per unit may vary considerably. As long as equal credit is given for easy or hard work, employees will choose what's easy.

For example, in the case of a word-processing pool, your incentive system may give equal credit for all word-processed pages regardless of whether they consist of a short letter, a long report, or just edited corrections. When productivity in measured in this way, people pick the easy jobs while the difficult ones sit, regardless of urgency. Or, in a warehousing operation, order pullers may get credit for orders pulled. Again, if the orders vary from one line to many, pullers will fight over who gets the easy ones.

Any time work is queued, workers have the option of picking and choosing what to do next.

Given more realistic measurements, the counterproductive effects will subside.

Excess Inventory

Production incentives may also lead employees to build as much as possible—which is fine when demand is unlimited. But when excess inventory winds up gathering dust in a warehouse, the company pays for debt, storage, insurance, and the other costs of carrying the items. Being forced to dump the inventory below cost may be all it takes to get managers to choose incentives geared toward meeting schedules or filling customer orders—and even eliminating the warehouse!

PURCHASING EVALUATION

Purchase price variance is the difference between standard or budgeted costs for materials and actual prices paid. A favorable variance results from buying at lower prices—often the result of volume discount. So when a purchasing department is evaluated on the basis of purchase price variance, excess inventory tends to build up. Management should initiate another evaluation approach introducing a scientific approach toward weighing order-quantity and carrying costs.

Unintended Markets

Just as production incentives cause workers to build excess inventory, commission systems often encourage salespeople to go after volume, without regard to profitability or the likelihood of collecting from the customer. But the sales force is just following motivations brought about by a poor system.

Even if salespeople are compensated for contributing to profits, traditional measuring systems may actually cause profits to diminish, since traditional methods undercost small, complex, or custom orders. Or salespeople in a job shop may direct all their orders to old, inefficient machinery because its fully depreciated condition makes the operation appear more profitable. The motivation toward profitable sales may be distorted by inaccurate measurements.

ABM System Implications

Unless you put enough thought into developing incentive systems, even ABM can lead to problems. For example, a common cost driver for purchasing costs is number of purchase orders. While the relationship may be reasonable for describing cost behavior, pressuring purchasing to reduce the number of orders may encourage employees to increase order quantities, resulting in excess inventories. As with purchase price variance, order costs are not balanced with carrying costs. So be careful. When using activity drivers to evaluate incentive systems, take a hard look at the unintended effects that might occur in motivating people, and find bases that properly relate costs to causes.

Modern Incentive Systems

To be successful, incentive systems must define meaningful ways of measuring progress. Your goal may be to reduce scrap or rework cost to a lower level. Or you may want to minimize tying up construction equipment at a site. Whatever needs improvement today should be the basis for incentive.

A modern approach to incentive systems includes team-level gainsharing. Individual incentives and sales commission systems must also adapt to today's needs.

Gainsharing

Gainsharing, a sharing of rewards by an entire team, differs from traditional incentive systems in that it includes the following important characteristics:

- ◆ Formation of direct labor groups or teams, with some latitude in the way operations are carried out
- ◆ Rewards, based on performance and how it is tied to increased profits, in which all members of the team share—and correspondingly, in which no rewards are given when targets cannot be met, as might occur in a business slowdown
- ◆ Ideally, evolving and changing measures of performance to reflect areas of greatest current concern and to ensure that operations do not become static

To elaborate, the degree of latitude given is up to management. Authority delegated should be sufficient to allow teams to collectively suggest and implement recommendations toward meeting their goals. No one is more intimately familiar with operations than the person who performs them, and employee involvement programs have had much documented success.

The reward should be shared; otherwise, people with little reason to help one another may pursue their own objectives to the detriment of others. One advantage of a team is that the strengths of one worker augment the weaknesses of another, which is why collectively, it can become a powerful force in any kind of improvement program.

Withholding rewards during a business downturn can help management avoid layoffs. Pay automatically adjusts.

Finally, performance measures must evolve along with operations. This ensures that improvement is continuous and that all problems are attacked. Many industries have become so competitive that running hard is necessary just to stay in place.

METALS COMPANY

For example, a metals company acquired out of bankruptcy has a traditional standards system. In an effort to turn the company around, management has drastically reduced fixed pay rates and in their place introduced departmental ABM-based productivity incentives that will be shared by everyone working on a shift.

Results: Although things start off slowly, productivity begins to turn around to where over 50 percent of direct labor compensation is incentive pay. Just a few short years later the company is among the most profitable in its industry.

A gainsharing system calls for key operating measures. When employees exceed targets, they share in the additional profits from the anticipated cost saving. But as indicated in the first portion of this chapter, the following measurements should be avoided for key indicators:

- Rewards for consumption
- Rewards for production, without reference to quality or need
- Measurements that consider dissimilar types of work to be the same
- Sales incentives that ignore profits or the ability of customers to pay their bills
- Measurements that are descriptive but that would lead to detrimental behavior if used to motivate improvement

Key indicators and their derivation are covered in the next chapter. For now, here are three of the more widely applicable ones that may be applied in service as well as manufacturing contexts:

1. Cost per unit of output
2. Rework
3. Customer satisfaction measures

Individual Incentives

While gainsharing is appropriate for creating team-level incentives, you still need some way to evaluate individuals for pay raises. Question and reexamine the traditional methods of evaluation, and avoid any system that tends to isolate workers. You may have to alter your culture to promote a new view of the worker. Individual incentives should be drawn from the company's overall objectives. Criteria should be specific but diverse enough to accommodate all desired personal development goals. Cross-training, for example, can be encouraged by evaluating and rewarding employees for the number of tasks they have mastered. Quality and operator maintenance are other objectives that may be evaluated.

Sales Commission Systems

Gainsharing for salespeople should be considered to the degree suitable. But even without it, you can substantially improve on traditional commission systems. The best ones reward according to *actual profit contribution*, i.e., when payment from the customer is received. This motivates your sales force to obtain profitable business from credit-worthy customers.

The system might also include volume as well as profit. By defining a budgeted gross profit range within which your salespeople receive normal commissions, you establish a system by which averaging above that range triggers additional incentives; averaging below it causes a penalty. At some point, you must establish a point of minimum profitability below which no credit is received toward commission.

To illustrate, let's say the normal range of gross profit determined under ABM is 37 to 43 percent and the normal commission rate is 5 percent, as shown in Exhibit 9-1. A salesperson averaging over 43 percent for a month receives a bonus to that month's commission as accounts receivable are collected. A salesperson averaging under 30 percent receives credit only if it is specially approved by management.

Implementation Considerations

The area of incentives should not be jumped into head first, particularly if no incentive system is presently in place. Unless employees will accept a cut in the fixed portion of their pay or a reduction in other benefits, implementation will have to proceed gradually. Under these circumstances, you should provide incentives only on improvements made after the date of system initiation.

I'll never forget the unfortunate experience of a new general manager of a chain of beauty clinics. She immediately set out to improve productivity by offering an incentive based on the number of treatments given per day, above and beyond base pay. Productivity did, in fact, increase, but it was more than offset by the additional labor cost to support the program.

Exhibit 9-1. Sample Sales Commission System

Average Gross Profit for Period	Commission
37–43%	5%
> 43%	5% + bonus
< 37%	5% − penalty
< 30%	None

Ideally, sales commissions are based on actual profits on cash collected. The amount of commission may vary with profit level. Below a certain minimum profitability, management approval should be required in order to obtain commission.

Incentive programs merit serious planning and consideration. Having an ABM system provides the best possible support for such programs, as it furnishes the detail and visibility necessary to assess the benefits.

Practical Pointers

♦ Any incentive system may have hidden, undesirable outcomes. Extreme care must be taken to avoid these pitfalls.
♦ Motivating people to move in the proper direction should begin by understanding what causes costs.

ABM's implications for design are covered in the next chapter.

10

The Right Data for
Product or Service Design

Not only does ABM help you eliminate waste and correctly motivate people, it benefits the design of your products and services—the very heart of your business.

As this chapter demonstrates, ABM can help you reexamine the many design aspects that affect your ability to take advantage of today's move toward customization in the most cost-effective way.

Product design determines product cost. In both manufacturing and service industries, the effects of design decisions can make or break the company and determine who wins and who loses in the marketplace. On the other hand, the incompatibility of designs with production facilities can create inefficiency. In clarifying trade-offs, ABM demonstrates how much design can affect cost.

The costs of poor designs are not limited to the designers themselves. They affect even those companies asked to produce to a design, e.g., job shops that manufacture to customer specifications or builders that construct according to architects' plans. Cost-estimating systems must consider these issues.

Trends in design of products and services provide additional cogent reasons for using ABM:

1. Increased customer focus
2. Broader definition of the product or service to encompass all important aspects, intangible as well as tangible
3. More emphasis on characteristics beyond low cost

In improving design, decisions should involve the following:

1. *Cross-functional participation, particularly by those responsible for carrying out the design in the production process.* ABM's common language can facilitate this.

2. *The most cost-effective approach in the context of design requirements.* ABM's focus on efficiency ensures its maximization.
3. *The most direct path to fulfilling customer needs.* The idea is compatible with ABM's visibility.

Review of the Design Process

Under traditional methods, engineers design products. Process engineering and planning operationalize design information after most design decisions relating to cost have been determined. Designs may call for:

1. Multiplicity of products
2. Too many parts
3. Expensive, scrap-laden, or difficult-to-work material
4. Too close of a tolerance

among other things.

Engineering change notices may proliferate to accommodate manufacturing problems not fully anticipated in design. In service industries, engineers may not be involved, but design decisions have no less of an impact. Corporate offices may dictate catering to certain preferences through corporate policies that may be resisted in the field. As in manufacturing design, operations must be involved from the start to ensure that goals can be met in an acceptable manner at minimum cost.

Using ABM in Design

Because ABM makes design trade-offs and decisions easily visible and understandable, costs of activities can be stated in terms of what drives them. The costs of complexity or poor design can then be dealt with by:

1. Redesigning the product
2. Utilizing resources more suitable to the design
3. Giving customers the option of an increase in price or a design change

Activities can be associated with specific bases intended to best reflect the underlying operation. Options highlighted by ABM include the following four actions: decreasing complexity, modularizing, defining services, and decreasing material costs.

Decreasing Complexity

As long as ABM pinpoints the relevant activity drivers, it provides the means for reducing complexity and its costs.

Assembly complexity, for example, affects purchasing, receiving, stocking, inspection, handling, and other activities classified as overhead as well as direct labor. Undercosting of particularly complex items may be obvious to operations, but buried in overhead by accounting. Unless ABM is implemented, the inability to formally document or communicate these costs is a major source of frustration. Under ABM, costs can follow the number of components assembled. Design may then reflect lower assembly costs as the number of components falls.

AUTOMOTIVE PARTS MANUFACTURER

Automotive Parts Manufacturer's two major product lines, motors and pumps, occupy opposite ends of the complexity spectrum. The company uses a process costing system made up of the two production departments applied on the basis of equivalent-units measures of output. Because sales of each line are roughly equal, service department costs, including scheduling, production control, purchasing, material handling, tooling, inspection, data entry, and related equipment, are split equally between the departments.

However, more and more business seems to be coming in for the complex motors, and business for the simpler pumps is waning. Margins overall begin to deteriorate. Management demands an explanation and turns to ABM.

Results: An ABM system is able to clarify the impact of additional complexity on profitability. The culprit turns out to be the cost system. Pricing for pumps is based on inflated costs, whereas motors are underpriced. Sales are increasing for the (low-priced) motors, but anticipated profits have not followed. The differential not reflected by the sales-volume–based allocation of service departments is complexity. Motors require six parts per dollar of material compared to one for pumps, and seven operations per dollar of labor compared to three for pumps. With differences of that magnitude, the sales-volume–based allocation of service department costs causes a great deal of distortion. When prices for quoting are adjusted to reflect actual costs, the company makes a comeback in the pumps market.

Modularizing

You may simplify products or services by modularizing, so one basic model may be completed with several options. This eliminates the need for an entirely separate product. ABM reflects simplification in decreased incurrence of product-line, lot-based, and other costs driven by manufacturing complexity.

Modularization means standardizing custom features. Efficiencies in manufacturing design can be attained despite customer demands.

A common example of this occurs in automobile manufacturing. Before Henry Ford introduced mass production, automobiles were produced to blueprint specifications, like houses. This technique failed to recognize all that the various end products had in common. In response to the costly inefficiency inherent in that type of process, today a base model is produced, to which may be added "modules," such as an air-conditioning system, a stereo, custom painting, or other features. These features may even be usable in other base models made by the same or other companies, encouraging volume production and lower prices for the modules. The base model is generically suited to accommodate all finishing touches. The process has been so designed that these decisions may wait until the final assembly stage, rather than in the initial stages of production. An efficient compromise is struck between pure customization and pure standardization.

Modularization reduces not only manufacturing costs but also forecast and inventory risks.

FURNITURE MAKER CORP.

Furniture Maker Corp., struggling to reduce costs, tries ABM.

Results: ABM reveals that the activity driver of number of component parts is responsible for much of the scheduling and inventory carrying costs. By modularizing products through the use of common legs, for example, inventory turns increase while paperwork diminishes.

Defining Services

Excess costs in service operations are caused by problems not contemplated in the design of routine service. The costs arise not from inefficiency but from a hazy definition of the service itself.

MORTGAGE BANKING CO.

Mortgage Banking Co. needs to raise servicing prices to recover higher operating costs. Most of the cost increase stems from noncompliance of certain borrowers with tax documentation requirements, financial statement submissions, or insurance standards. Other costs arise from preparing special reports for certain investors. When the situation is brought to management's attention, the inequity of the charges become clear: Good customers are suffering from higher servicing prices through the fault of careless ones.

Results: Instead of spreading the price increase over all loans, management decides to redesign the fee schedule to reflect costs for the services it is intended to perform. Problems caused by customers are now charged back to them. When they feel the impact of their noncompliance, the problems disappear. The end result is reduced costs overall and higher profitability without an across-the-board price increase.

Decreasing Material Costs

Beyond activity decisions, material alternatives are rampant. Coil steel generally costs less than sheet. Using forgings or castings instead of raw steel reduces the need for machining. These alternatives are best considered while product design is still fluid.

TROPHY MANUFACTURER

Trophy Manufacturer sells to dealers through a catalog that lists stock products plus offers for custom items. Stock designs of a man with an outstretched arm or of a galloping horse with its tail in the air have definite weaknesses: The small protrusions may be fragile and break during tumbling operations for vacuum plating. Yet traditional cost records may give no indication of the extra breakage cost. Management calls for further investigation.

Results: Results of ABM analysis are quite shocking: Items scrapped out of loss of these appendages are included in an overhead pool spread evenly over all products. If, instead, the scrap costs are applied to the products causing them, the opportunity for cost reduction becomes visible. Through a combination of simpler design and more durable material, the loss is eliminated.

Before new design ideas can reach their full potential, an accounting system adequate to support decisions must be implemented. ABM is that system.

Compendium I
Key Cost-Cause Indicators

Here are some key activity drivers and other statistics that have proved useful in controlling costs and improving operations. As with everything else, not all statistics are suitable for all situations. To improve efficiency, choose a few factors, ones that will work best in your business.

Efficiency: Key Statistics

General

General measures indicate progress toward goals of timely service, flexibility, inventory reduction, cash flow, and myriad other characteristics associated with healthy businesses.

A. Throughput
   - For order environments, days from receipt of order to shipment. This can also be effectively subdivided into its various component times.
   - For stock environments, inventory levels provide a similar measure.
B. Production lead time
   - Days' cost of sales in work-in-process
   - Percentage of process to total elapsed time from order to shipment
   - Order backlog statistics
C. Productivity
   - Output per unit of input, measured in dollars or activity-driver statistics; e.g., cost per unit of output. The statistic must control for quality and should consider need.
D. Design efficiency
   - Activity-driver quantities per end product (e.g., number of components, footage, weight, etc.)

    E. Costs of quality
- Accumulation of costs and statistics from varying sources, including internal functions, scrap, rework, returns, and so on

Labor

Here are four major categories of labor to be watched under any system. With detailed time reporting, additional measures may be found meaningful. But care should be taken not to measure labor to the minute, as some traditional systems do, to the neglect of the far more significant material and overhead categories.

    A. Overtime
- Overtime premium paid, with causes
- Unforeseen overtime
- Overtime chargeable to customers

    B. Downtime
- Downtime incurred, with causes

    C. Rework
- Rework performed, with causes
- Chargeable rework

    D. Special skills
- Underapplied skills and dollar effects

Material and Inventory

The efficiency with which material and inventory are handled may be assessed by various key statistics, as follows.

    A. Vendor performance
- Vendor evaluations

    B. Scrap
- Defect rate, by cause
- Off-fall as a percentage to material used

    C. Shrinkage
- Book-to-physical adjustment
- Cycle or periodic test-count differences

    D. Material handling
- Number of moves per routing

    E. Inventory-carrying costs
- Inventory turns

           ◆ Inventory aging
           ◆ Inventory-carrying cost rate
      F. Substitution of material
           ◆ Number of substitutions and dollar effects

Automation

      A. Machine setup
           ◆ Number of setups
           ◆ Cost or time per setup
      B. Overautomation
           ◆ The relationship between asset additions and depreciation expense—a general gauge for determining whether automation is ahead or behind needs
      C. Bottlenecks
           ◆ Queue at the bottleneck
      D. Maintenance
           ◆ Unscheduled breakdowns
           ◆ Time that machines are in service
      E. Tooling optimization
           ◆ Breakdowns or time lost from need to change tooling during runs
      F. Idle capacity costs
           ◆ Measure of utilized to available capacity

Administrative Functions

      A. General
           ◆ Cost per unit of activity driver
           ◆ Rework rate
      B. Order costs
           ◆ Costs per order or order line

Customer Costs

      A. General
           ◆ Special service costs, by customer
      B. Costs of extending credit
           ◆ Ratio of collection to sales, by type of customer
      C. Marketing and advertising
           ◆ Sales dollar collected per advertising dollar spent, by medium

Customer Service: Key Statistics

As important as efficiency and cost management is customer service. Today, the focus of production and services is on meeting the customers' needs. The following are examples of some indicators that might be used.

- A. General Service
  - Level of work in process
  - Survey results
  - Customer complaints and returns
  - Customer turnover
- B. Pricing
  - Bids lost
- C. Delivery
  - Comparison of date promised to actual
  - Open orders past due
  - Orders expedited
- D. Stockouts
  - Number
  - Time out of stock

Compendium II
Checklists, Forms, and Rules of Thumb to Help You Track Costs

Implementation Checklists

Recap of the Five Steps to Designing and Implementing ABM

See chapter 3 of the text for details.

- A. Develop a resource usage path.
- B. Assign costs, level I.
- C. Assign costs, level II.
- D. Budget drivers and relate to costs.
- F. Validate the model.

Five Steps to Cost Management: A Shortcut to Getting Started

- A. *Prepare a resource usage path for your organization.* Involve a cross-functional team representative of operations. Start with identifying the major activities, and then consider what drives them.
- B. *Have your accountant determine the numbers, including activity costs and driver quantities.* If he or she gives you a blank look, provide Chapters 2 and 3. At this stage, estimates are preferable to no data at all.
- C. *Analyze your most significant activities.* Think about near-term goals for controlling costs. Consider what is most controllable. Your options include reducing workload and better matching workload

with capacity. You can reduce workload by decreasing demands in the form of activity-driver quantities or the cost per activity driver.

D. *Develop key statistics covering these activities for your organization.* See Compendium I for ideas. Supplement the statistics with connections to performance evaluation and incentives. Assign teams and give employees latitude.

E. *Watch what happens.* Attaining one goal leads to another. Never stop improving!

Three Steps to Controlling Project Costs

A. *Planning.* Develop an estimate based on activity costs and activity drivers. Chart out in detail how you expect to progress and how you will attain your goals. Gauge actual against planned performance.

B. *Control.* Attain at anytime up-to-date information:
   - Actual versus estimated activity drivers.
   - Costs incurred versus budget based on activity drivers actually incurred to date, to provide a measure of completion. Here, the budget can be interpreted as value added to date.
   - Comparison of actual progress to scheduled completion dates.
   - Discretionary costs, including overtime and rework.

C. *Postcompletion.* Evaluate how the project went and what it indicates about long-term capabilities. Focus on improving results in the future.

Forms

Cost-Cause Grid Format

The first step in ABM implementation is documenting the cost-cause relationships in your organization. This should be done as shown in Exhibit CII-1. Once complete, the grids may be summarized into support, discretionary, direct, or special requirements activities and entered into the resource usage path.

Resource Usage Path Format

This is the final design stage document. From here, actual costs and drivers are added. The result is an ABM model customized to suit your operation's information needs. See Exhibit CII-2.

Exhibit CII-1. Cost-Cause Grid Format

Activity Drivers ("Cause")	Activities ("Cost")
◆	
◆	
◆	
◆	
◆	
◆	
◆	
◆	
◆	
◆	

Rules of Thumb

ABM Implementation

A. *Level of detail.* If an activity makes up less than one or 2 percent of the total for the reporting unit, combine it with other similar activities for purposes of cost application and analysis. The idea is to reduce complexity to the lowest acceptable level while retaining realism. Otherwise, you risk getting lost in details that do not affect results significantly.

B. *Averaging vs. activity driving.* When you divide costs by activity drivers, it seems like averaging. For example, purchasing costs are "averaged" over the number of orders for an "average" cost per order. While this is true to a degree, it misses the purpose of ABM. If costs per unit of driver are roughly the same, averaging is appropriate; if not, you need to identify additional activity drivers to remove the variance. For example, you may have to use setup time instead of number of setups as an activity driver if the variation between types of setups is large. A rule of thumb is that variation within 10 percent or so of an average is acceptable.

C. *Order of cost assignment at level I.* Start with the support center that affects the largest number of other support centers. Employee benefits, maintenance, or occupancy could qualify. Once that cen-

Exhibit CII-2. Resource Usage Path Format

| Level I Drivers | Support Activities | Level II Drivers | Operating Activities | | Costs |

Resource Usage
End products/services
Inventories
Cost of sales
Operating expenses

Discretionary

Support

- Discretionary

- Specific customers, orders, services, products

ter's costs have been fully assigned, move on to the center affecting the next largest number of support centers. If crossover is significant, determine those assignments simultaneously, e.g., a maintenance department that consumes occupancy costs but also contributes to the occupancy cost pool by providing janitorial or grounds services.

D. *Complexity factors.* Complexity factors can help you to do a better job in associating activity drivers and activities. For example, activity costs may be driven by both footage and gauge of coiled metal. In that case, you may separate cost per foot by light, medium, and heavy gauge; or, use a complexity factor. You can substitute a factor as long as it is explicitly defined and understood by users of the system.

E. *Fractional resource saving.* The only satisfactory solution to the fractional resource saving controversy is to consider capacity. Resources that were once occupied with inefficiency are available to use elsewhere. Joe can use the extra two hours created by the new efficiency to perform preventive maintenance, study setups, or do the hundred-odd other projects that he currently may not have time to do. Ultimately, combining functions may be possible.

Twelve Critical Areas for ABM Focus

While every business can benefit from an ABM system, certain red flags may indicate a more urgent need to change from poor existing systems. Certain operating elements require sophisticated costing. Characteristics to consider are as follows:

A. *Distinct lines of business.* A dilemma arising in traditional accounting is how to determine profitability of two or more distinct lines of business; this is because of the system's focus on contribution to corporate overhead. Recall the situations of the electric motor repair and distribution company and of the diversified manufacturer. Traditional techniques cannot address the issue. Only ABM can uncover which operations are truly profitable.

B. *Distinct customer or distribution channels.* Variety in customers or distribution channels is another operational aspect not handled adequately by traditional costing. Recall the situation of the awards manufacturer who sells through retail as well as distribution channels, and that of the gaming distributor who sells to distinct national and local accounts. Say the manufacturer has been presented with an opportunity for additional retail business. Its present system, based entirely on standard manufacturing costs, fails to address distribution channel profitability. ABM is needed to assess the desirability of the offer.

C. *Small and large orders.* An issue related to customers is variation in order sizes. Because certain costs are incurred by the order regardless of size, overhead generated by small orders is likely to be disproportionate to revenue earned. Although special studies may be conducted under traditional costing, their results are suspect because the model is only partial and not compared to actual. Only ABM can determine the amount of small-order overhead for costing on an ongoing basis. The need for special studies disappears.

D. *High- and low-volume products.* High- and low-volume products often involve simple and complex processing, respectively. Complex processing generates additional overhead, which traditional systems do not reflect. Additional overhead may take the form of scrap, rework, supervision, or other costs, such as those for special materials. Operating managers seem to recognize the inaccuracy of complex-item profitability intuitively. Reconciliation of costing and intuition follows from ABM implementation. Situations like this one may turn operating managers into ABM's strongest advocates.

E. *Custom and stock operations.* The inadequacies of traditional accounting may become evident through its bias toward custom work, which runs contrary to the intuition of operations. Custom work appears to beat stock items in profitability, and the more complex the better. As a company moves toward more of that sort of work, expected profits may not materialize. Implementation of ABM can provide the accuracy missing from traditional cost systems, and operating managers are proved correct once more.

F. *Introduction of new technology.* Traditional costing does not contemplate technological changes. Although they know it's wrong, accountants will cost new technology in the old way, because that's the only way that seems to be available. When new technology is introduced, a red flag appears, indicating a high probability that products are being miscosted. Under ABM, in contrast, costing adapts to suit the new operation.

G. *Alternate manual and automated routings within a department.* The significance of having alternate automated and manual routings within a department is that traditional systems generally cost both the same way, e.g., labor times a burden rate or cost per equivalent unit produced. Having differing cost systems within a single department is almost unknown. The distortion is particularly prone to occur when alternate methods are relatively new. Under ABM, the focus instead is on activities, not departments. Distinct routings can be accounted for in the manner that is most suitable.

H. *Line- or machine-paced operations.* Traditional job-cost methods in particular do not accommodate any basis for assigning conversion costs other than to direct labor time. While accountants may undergo various types of contortions in an effort to make it work, retaining labor as the base simply does not fit line- or machine-paced operations. The presence of modern operations almost automatically indicates that a labor time-based system is inadequate.

I. *Underutilized or unutilized operations.* Low utilization is a sign that an operation may potentially be overcosted, discouraging increased utilization. Recall the case of Machinery-Maker Corp. from Chapter 7. Improper accounting for idle capacity from outsourcing results in more outsourcing, more idle capacity, and even higher costs per labor hour. The company loses more and more money in a hopeless downward spiral. Normalization of fixed costs may be required: Costs are determined over normal capacity, and unabsorbed costs are charged to idle capacity.

K. *Bottlenecks.* Traditional costing seldom recognizes the detrimental effects of bottlenecks. Operations can only suspect the actual dollar impact that bottlenecks may have. Through ABM, you can trace costs to the bottlenecks that cause them. As illustrated in the Bar Splitter Ltd. example in Chapter 11, the once hidden effects can be devastating.

L. *Lot-based operations.* Assuming all costs are unit-level, traditional costing does not provide separate accounting for lot-based operations, such as immersion for plating, order processing, material handling, or other operations. If computed on labor time, costs applied are unlikely to equal actual costs. Many systems relegate the entire operation to an overhead pool applied over chargeable time of other operations. Under ABM, recognition of lot-based costs allows costing to make better sense.

M. *Chargeable special services.* Special services provided as extras are unlikely to be well accounted for in traditional settings. Rather, the costs tend to be averaged over all output. ABM classifies them as special requirements activities, and segregates them in costing and reporting.

Part II

ABM in Action:
Practical Applications

11

Case Studies and Their Cost-Cause Models

We now turn to an in-depth look at eight diverse applications of ABM information. (If you need help getting started with ABM and are looking for a relevant industry example, you are likely to find one in Chapter 4.) They are as follows:

1. Breakeven
2. New product vs. old
3. Costs in common in real estate
4. Pricing and valuing a business
5. Bottlenecks
6. Complexity
7. Make-or-buy
8. Equipment leasing

Breakeven

Introduced in the discussion accompanying Exhibit 7-3 only as an insourcing consideration, breakeven analysis has much wider applications. In traditional accounting, breakeven is the volume level at which variable profit equals fixed costs, while under ABM, it helps determine the revenue or profit level that will fully cover costs associated with activity drivers.

Many industries use this type of analysis: Hotels state it as a certain occupancy rate; real estate developers apply a multiplier to land cost to determine a breakeven selling price for what's built; in education, it means maintenance of a certain student-to-faculty ratio. ABM challenges these old rules of thumb against current facts and circumstances: Are the assumptions grounded in the facts, and are they always true for all operations?

Steel Service Companies

An area of major concern in steel service companies is the disposition of off-fall material. Under an ABM system, costs of reprocessing this material may appear radically different from those shown by a traditional one. By now, you should be familiar with this type of operation. The cost-cause grid for its direct activities is presented in Exhibit 11-1.

Under the traditional costing method shown in Exhibit 11-2, conversion costs are applied to products on the basis of pounds. An off-fall coil weighing 1,000 pounds would be applied correspondingly lower costs than a master coil weighing 10,000 pounds. Assuming that the cost of the material per pound is the same and that an equal portion of each coil is scrapped, the runs show the same margin. In this exhibit, a per-pound selling price of $0.35 and a cost of $0.27 gives equal profits of $0.08.

The ABM approach illustrated in Exhibits 11-3 and 11-4 recognizes the activities more appropriately. Activities required to process the two coils are very similar, despite the difference in weight: Both coils require setup, and both are of equal length and gauge; because of the equal lengths, both tie up the slitting machinery an equal amount of time; both require order processing and shipping costs.

As a result, processing the off-fall coil actually generates a loss, bringing into question whether a policy of retaining certain off-fall for reprocessing is desirable. Unless a lower-cost slitter made especially for

Exhibit 11-1. Cost-Cause Grid for a Steel Service Company

Level II Drivers ("Cause")	Operating Activities ("Cost")
	Direct
◆ Orders	Order activities
◆ Turret/other setups	Slitting setup
◆ Footage, gauge	Slitting run
◆ Direct charge	Leftover material
◆ Master coils	Material handling
◆ Pallets	Packaging
◆ Asset value	Asset carrying
◆ Direct charge	Expected scrap, rework
◆ Customers	Customer activities
◆ Products	Tooling and design

Exhibit 11-2. Traditional Approach: Sample Steel Service Estimating Form

Description	Rate	Usage	Cost
Full Coil Extension:			
Raw material	.20/lb.	10,000	$2,000
Yield loss	4%	400	
Scrap recovery	.05/lb.	(400)	(20)
Subtotal		9,600	1,980
Conversion costs	.06/lb.	9,600	576
Total		9,600	$2,556
Drop Coil Extension:			
Raw material	.20/lb.	1,000	$200
Yield loss	4%	40	
Scrap recovery	.05/lb.	(40)	(2)
Subtotal		960	198
Conversion costs	.06/lb.	960	58
Total		960	$256

	Full Coil Extension	Drop Coil Extension
Total cost	$2,556	$256
Total pounds	9,600	960
Cost per pound	$.27	$.27
Selling price per pound	$.35	$.35
Net profit (loss) per pound	$.08	$.08

The approach shown here is a process approach that uses pounds as the equivalent unit. Processing a narrow off-fall coil *appears* to generate as much profit as processing a master coil. As will become clear, basing costs on pounds distorts profitability perceptions significantly.

processing the narrow-width drop coils can be utilized through insourcing or outsourcing, the policy would seem to verge on suicide.

Profitability by product line is reflected in Exhibit 11-5. Whereas traditional approaches tend to average in drops with heavy- and light-gauge categories, ABM highlights the *effects* of the drops. Here is yet another example of how costing can impact decision making.

Exhibit 11-3. ABM Approach: Sample Steel Service Estimating Form

Description	Rate	Usage	Cost
Full Coil Extension:			
Material and coil costs:			
Raw material	$.20/lb.	10,000	$2,000
Material handling	$50/coil	1	50
Setup	$65/setup	1	65
Subtotal			$2,115
Yield loss	4%	400	
Scrap recovery	$.05/lb.	(400)	(20)
Subtotal, all orders		9,600	$2,095
Less material required order		9,600	
Leftover material		0	
Apply to other orders		0	
Chargeable leftover		0	
Minus scrap recovery		0	
Subtotal, this order		0	$2,095
Processing and other services:			
Slitting, light gauge	$.10 ft.	2,800	$ 280
Less portion charged to others			0
Order activities	$50/order	1	50
Shipping	$20/pallet	1	20
Special requirements			0
Risks, rework, downtime	$.01/ft.	2,800	28
TOTAL			$2,473
Drop Coil Extension:			
Material and coil costs:			
Raw material	.20/lb.	1,000	$200
Material handling	$50/coil	1	50
Setup	$65/setup	1	65
Subtotal			$315
Yield loss	4%	40	
Scrap recovery	.05/lb.	(40)	(2)
Subtotal, all orders		960	$313
Less material required		960	
Leftover material		0	

Description	Rate	Usage	Cost
Drop Coil Extension:			
Material and coil costs:			
Apply to other orders		0	
Chargeable leftover		0	
Minus scrap recovery		0	
Subtotal, this order		0	$313
Processing and other services:			
Slitting, light gauge	.10 ft.	2,800	280
Less portion charged to others			0
Order activities	$50/order	1	50
Shipping	$20/pallet	1	20
Special requirements			0
Risks, rework, downtime	.01/ft.	2,800	28
TOTAL			$691

	Full Coil Extension	*Drop Coil Extension*
Total cost	$2,473	$691
Total pounds	9,600	960
Cost per pound	$.26	$.72
Selling price per pound	$.35	$.35
Net profit (loss) per pound	$.09	($.37)

The results of ABM cannot be compared to those of the traditional model. As indicated, at some point it may be unprofitable to attempt to reprocess leftover material, because a large portion of total costs are driven by characteristics other than coil weight. Here, selling the 1,000-pound drop coil for scrap yields $.05 per pound compared to a loss of $.37. Even if scrap rather than full cost is used for the raw material, total cost decreases by only $150, which still produces a loss on a per-pound basis of $.21 per pound. A breakeven calculation is shown in Exhibit 11-6.

Exhibit 11-4. Derivation of ABM Model: Sample Steel Service Estimating Form

Activity Driver	Activity Cost	Budgeted Activity Drivers	Costing Rate
Raw material/pounds	n/a	direct charge	$.20
Material handling/coils	$250,000	5,000	$50.00
Setup/setups	250,000	3,846	$65.00
Percentage yield loss/pounds	n/a	direct charge	4%
Scrap recovery/pounds	n/a	direct charge	$.05
Slitting light/footage	400,000	4,000,000	$.10
Order activities/orders	150,000	3,000	$50.00
Shipping/pallets	300,000	15,000	$20.00
Special requirements	n/a	direct charge	various
Risks/footage	$40,000	4,000,000	$.01

Through budgeted activity costs and driver quantities, ABM determines costing rates per unit of driver. These rates form the basis for budgeting as well as the estimating form illustrated in Exhibit 11-3.

Recap of Steps in ABM Analysis

To review, the costing model illustrated in Exhibit 11-5 was constructed using the following steps:

1. *Develop a resource usage path.* Steel Service Co. needs to gain an understanding of the operation, including all salient aspects that affect costing. The significance of lot-based operations, scrap, leftover or drop material, and special customer services are notable. Direct centers include slitting, material handling, and pallet making/packaging. Setup, generation of leftover material, and run activities can be distinguished within the slitting direct center, for which the activity drivers of setups, direct charge, and footage may be associated, respectively. Similarly, other direct centers and activities are associated with their appropriate drivers. The supporting centers to be assigned include supervision, maintenance, occupancy, personnel, employee benefits, and miscellaneous.

2. *Assign costs, level I.* The company reorganizes financial data to fit the activity structures just defined. At level I, the supporting centers iden-

Exhibit 11-5. Steel Service Product-Line Profitability

Activity Driver	Light Gauge	Heavy Gauge	Drops
Activity-driver quantities (000):			
Raw material	50,000/lb.	50,000/lb.	20,000/lb.
Material handling	6.0/coil	5.0/coil	5.5/coil
Setup	4.0	3.0	5.0
Yield loss	2,200/lb.	2,300/lb.	2,200/lb.
Scrap recovery	2,200/lb.	2,300/lb.	2,200/lb.
Slitting light gauge	14,400/ft.		13,300/ft.
Slitting heavy gauge/feet	—	2,900/ft.	2,400/ft.
Order activities	3.0/order	2.7/order	3.5/order
Shipping	9.0/pallet	10.0/pallet	6.0/pallet
Extended Costs (000):			
Raw material ($\times$ .20)	$10,000	$10,000	$4,000
Material handling ($\times$ 50)	300	250	275
Setup ($\times$ 65)	260	195	325
Scrap recovery ($\times$ .05)	(110)	(115)	(110)
Slitting light ($\times$ .10)	1,440	—	1,330
Slitting heavy ($\times$ .14)	—	406	336
Order activities ($\times$ 50)	150	135	175
Shipping ($\times$ 20)	180	200	120
Total	$12,220	$11,071	$6,451
Net pounds sold	47,800	47,700	17,800
Cost per pound	$.26	$.23	$.36
Average selling price	$.30	$.30	$.30
Net profit (loss)	$.04	$.07	($.06)
Conversion cost per pound sold	$.05	$.02	$.14

As illustrated here, the conversion cost per pound sold is much higher on average when reprocessing drop coils. Because losses are anticipated in reprocessing, excesses over recoverable market value should be charged back to orders responsible for generating the drops. If recalculated assuming only $.05 scrap value as material cost, as done in the explanation for Exhibit 11-3, drop reprocessing as a product line is generally profitable. While earnings on drop reprocessing may be sufficient to exceed outright sale of scrap, this is a clearly less profitable use of resources. Profit produced per minute is lower.

Note that for simplicity, the same raw material cost of $.20 was assumed for both light- and heavy-gauge raw material.

tified are assigned to direct centers and the activities within them. Actual costs should be modified to future-oriented budgets, intended to represent current instead of historical operations.

3. *Assign costs, level II.* Activity costs are pooled and assigned to activity drivers. For direct activities, the result is the "activity cost" column of Exhibit 11-4. Note that discretionary and other nonassigned costs are excluded from the exhibit, with the exception of general downtime and rework risks, which you might include in the model according to user preference.

4. *Budget drivers and relate them to costs.* Activity-driver budgets are determined. The most efficient way to derive the budgets is to explode budgeted end items through a bill of activity. Alternatively (in this example), you could convert into footage the pounds information that is readily available from the system. The result is the "budgeted activity drivers" column in Exhibit 11-4.

5. *Set up flexible budgets to validate the model, using the costing rate per unit of activity driver.* These rates feed directly into support of all ABM applications. Decisions regarding efficiency, product design, outsourcing, incentives, and pricing draw directly from this information.

Having all of this information finally available, Steel Service Co. needs a way to generalize its results to formulate a new policy to stop the off-fall problem. It decides to determine a breakeven level, below which drop coil processing is automatically disallowed as unprofitable. The calculation is provided in Exhibit 11-6.

With the new tool of ABM in hand, operations eliminate most of the unprofitable processing that formerly went on. Capacity is freed up for profitable work. Through new marketing efforts, the company turns itself around.

New Product vs. Old

Changes in technology frequently result in processes that are so different that they can be only remotely likened to old methods. The output of these new technologies, if of adequate quality, may begin to replace the old and dominate the marketplace.

When operations change so radically, costing must keep pace. Management needs to analyze outputs, determine efficiencies, and identify chargeable customer services to keep an adequate handle on costs.

One industry subject to this kind of change is printing. The printing industry is highly competitive, emphasizing high service levels at reasonable cost. As is typical of job shops, printers are organized into functional layouts. Major departments include letterpress and lithography. Labor skill levels are high.

Printers are often viewed as prime candidates for detailed cost systems because they must be able to bid on unique jobs. Time is the measure of production, whether by machine or labor. Setup is significant. Cost systems are organized on a job-cost basis. To ensure that estimating is being done properly, costing includes frequent detailed comparisons of actual to estimate.

Graphic Arts Co. Example

One portion of the printing industry that is currently experiencing radical change is graphic arts, which prepares color photos or artwork for printing. The capabilities of personal computers and other prepress imaging technologies have transformed what were until recently heavily manual operations into computerized ones. Graphic Arts Co. faces a situation in which automation has replaced a traditionally labor-intensive process.

Up to the 1980s, the typical routing of a graphic arts order was photographing, stripping, proofing, and platemaking. Stripping positioned film in the order required for platemaking, and proofing provided proofs for review. The process required a highly skilled workforce and certain specialized materials, but little equipment. Under these circumstances, a traditional job-costing approach, with modifications described below, may have been adequate.

But the introduction of prepress imaging equipment automated the process: Scanners can now translate images to film; various costly electronic systems perform stripping, retouching, and color correction, whereas less demanding work is handled by microcomputer; operations are uniformly machine-paced rather than labor-paced, immediately rendering traditional job-cost systems obsolete.

While admitting that its cost system needs change, management of Graphic Arts Co. thinks a time-based system might still be adequate. Because tasks vary so widely, time may be the only short-term alternative. Although it is true that a multirate-machine, time-driven, job-cost system might work, ABM's multiple bases would still be an improvement. To use time as a base, you must take care to ensure that significant level I assignments are proper. For example:

Exhibit 11-6. Steel Service Breakeven Analysis

Assumptions:
Sales price: $.35
Scrap recovery value: $.05
Drop coil length: 2,800 ft.
Processing costs: See Exhibit 11-4.

Breakeven weight calculation:
Net contribution per pound

Sales price	$.350
Times yield rate	90%
Subtotal	$.315
Plus scrap recovery (.05 × 10% loss)	(.005
Subtotal	$.320
Less profit from scrapping	(.050)
TOTAL	$.270

Conversion costs to be recovered:

1 handling	50
1 setup	65
2,800 light footage	308
1 order	50
1 pallet	20
Total	$493

Breakeven calculation:

Conversion costs to be recovered	493.00
Divided by net contribution per pound	.27
Result	1,826 lbs.

Proof of breakeven weight calculation:

Revenue (1,826 × .90 × .35)	$575
Costs:	
Conversion	$493
Scrap recovery (1,826 × .10 × .05)	(9)
Scrap value (1,826 × .05)	91
Total	$575

As illustrated here, you can easily derive a breakeven weight from the assumptions listed. Net contribution per pound comes from $.35 received from the customer at a 90% yield rate, plus scrap recovery on the remaining 10% of material. To make processing worthwhile, revenue must exceed costs by at least $.05, representing the amount that could be received for scrap without further processing. This figure is subtracted from total revenue and scrap recovery to obtain $.27, the relevant amount. This is divided into the $493 total nonscrap conversion costs that must be recovered.

• *Inefficiencies such as downtime, rework, and overtime premiums* should not be averaged in computed rates. Ideally, these costs would be charged only against the orders causing them. If downtime is attributable to lack of work, or rework is due to internal failure, these costs are discretionary and reported separately from the costs of services sold.

• Similarly, *initial visits to customers who require additional service* should not be averaged over all current production but rather treated as a customer cost.

• *Indirect labor and supervision* should be assigned to the cost centers that cause the costs, particularly where only some centers have working supervisors.

• *Material-related overhead*, such as requisitioning, purchasing, and handling, should not be charged on the basis of labor but to material-intensive centers that generate the costs.

• *Administrative costs* should be related to cost-center head count, customer orders, or other bases.

• *Delivery charges* should reflect realistic variations in time and distance.

Assuming full ABM implementation, direct activities are illustrated in the cost-cause grid shown in Exhibit 11-7. For prepress imaging, machine time is acceptable until timing can be standardized through the bases suggested. For job costing, management should substitute a computer log for time cards. Under labor time-reporting systems, many issues characteristic of the new equipment's machine time may be missed. For example:

• The equipment may run unattended. Film may be produced during the night, or a particularly long microcomputer run may span two days. Using labor time as a base amounts to giving the services of the equipment away.

• The impact of run time differs depending on the equipment. Scanner operators may be able to set up the next job while the current one is running. On the other hand, microcomputer operators may be idle. While in theory, time is chargeable to the order, reporting should highlight it as avoidable downtime. Implementing a file server or dedicating a workstation to performing run tasks would reduce or eliminate the downtime.

Exhibit 11-7. Cost-Cause Grid: Graphic Arts Co.

Level II Drivers ("Cause")	Operating Activities ("Cost")
	Direct
◆ Orders	Order activities
◆ Direct charge	Material and labor
◆ Time, setups, film pieces, exposures, complexity	Manual processing
◆ Machine time; or setups, scans, film inches, images, complexity	Automated prepress imaging

◆ Because of the tendency of highly skilled labor to cross over to different departments, labor and equipment costs should be applied separately through different bases.

◆ Stage I assignment should adequately reflect the energy and maintenance requirements of the equipment.

◆ With the introduction of major equipment, normalization of fixed overhead rates on underutilized equipment is necessary.

Defining and relating time requirements to activity drivers add a new dimension to estimating and control. Hourly costing rates can be tied to underlying operations. Management can view cost on an activity-driver basis as well as according to time expended, giving management the information shown in Exhibit 11-8. Here, item characteristics drive costs of the new automated operations and old manual ones differently. This facilitates weighing of alternatives.

Costs in Common in Real Estate

Real estate has many unique characteristics that costing should reflect. Developers of commercial buildings who retain ownership and rent space upon completion might consider the following:

◆ *Common-area costs.* These costs include areas used by tenants but not part of their leased space, e.g., a conference room for tenants of an office building. Most of the time, commercial lessors charge common-area costs back to tenants. Because of this, the costs might not seem to be prime candidates for cost control. In today's competitive environment, however, this viewpoint may no longer be viable, as the case study will show.

◆ *Central administration.* In some ways similar to common-area costs, administration is sometimes treated as simply "there," and not related back as it should be on the basis of actual activities performed. Traditional accounting encourages this treatment by basing costs on irrelevant criteria, such as gross rentals.

◆ *Depreciation.* Unlike equipment, for real property, including land and buildings, depreciation has meaning only for tax purposes. The underlying property is usually appreciating in value. Any improvements or major repairs are capitalized and depreciated separately. Therefore, in the analysis, debt obligations are more significant.

◆ *Fixed costs and normalization.* Many costs, such as real estate taxes and insurance, are "fixed," regardless of the level of rent volume attained. Total rents must cover debt service and fixed costs; the rest is profit. With only one tenant, should the landlord set the rent level high enough to cover all depreciation, maintenance, insurance, and taxes? It is highly unlikely that the prospective tenant would agree to that. Take motels. Their pricing cannot fluctuate to cover the high costs of low occupancy during slow periods. In fact, the pricing tends to be just the opposite: Off-season discounts are offered to raise occupancy. Instead, the idea is to "normalize" cost so that costs relate to their drivers.

These issues are highlighted in the following case.

LOTS IN COMMON LTD.

Lots in Common Ltd. has many common-area amenities for its commercial tenants, including a fitness room, snack room, and child-care center. These facilities are so situated, however, that only a few tenants use them. Moreover, the company finds it necessary to raise rents at a rate faster than inflation to cover its ever-increasing central administrative office burden.

Management begins to realize the problems this is creating as tenants are choosing not to renew their leases. Vacancies in commercial properties are not easy to fill. Management looks to ABM.

Exhibit 11-8. Graphic Arts Co.: New vs. Old Product Cost

For the most common type of project:

Description	Quality Level Required		
	Low	Moderate	High
Conventional method:			
Strip	$ 50	$ 75	$100
Contact	25	40	60
Proof	35	50	100
Total	$110	$165	$260
Desktop method:			
Setup, input	$ 40	$ 90	N/A
Imaging	30	90	N/A
Total	$ 70	$180	N/A
High-end prepress imaging:			
Setup, input	$100	$100	$100
Imaging	100	100	100
Total	$200	$200	$200

As illustrated here, although the company has three alternative means of producing the same standard item, the quality of work required in the end product heavily determines cost. Where a low-quality image is called for, the desktop method provides the least costly process; for a high-quality image, on the other hand, the high-end prepress imaging equipment is best. Between the two extremes, the manual process wins out. As new technology is introduced in the industry, these results are likely to change from year to year.

Results: ABM enables management to identify its major categories of activities as follows:

◆ *Leasing.* Leasing means obtaining tenants to fill vacant space. For Lots in Common, the cost is paid as a commission on gross rental. Tenant turnover is the activity driver.

◆ *Common-area activities.* Common-area activities include mainte- nance, utilities, and other associated costs. Some of these may be

> driven by usage, others by time, e.g., weekly lawn mowing and nightly cleaning, and others are fixed.
>
> ◆ *Administration.* Most administrative functions are transaction-driven. For example, lease accounting varies according to the number of leases.

The analysis helps the company eliminate inefficiency and gain a handle on managing costs. Here are some of what becomes highlighted under ABM:

- ◆ Certain inefficiencies resulted from habitual overtime and the use of manual information systems. ABM pinpointed these for correction.
- ◆ Much administrative effort was generated by servicing a building in an outlying area. The profitability of this property is now visible.
- ◆ The company began to base common-area charges on utilization. As it turned out, the tenants who dominated the facilities were willing to pay for them.

The changes brought about by ABM are part of putting tenants' needs first. By eliminating excessive charges, the company could retain tenants and avoid vacancy and tenant recruitment costs.

Pricing and Valuing a Business

As an ABM consultant, I am frequently called upon to apply ABM principles to businesses being purchased or sold. I am often asked to answer questions like:

- ◆ How do my production efficiency and costs compare to theirs?
- ◆ Will the new operation turn a profit?
- ◆ How much capital will be required?

If you are asking the same questions, you may refer to data that are historical or from comparable operations. The ABM approach is the same: Design a model and test how predictive it is using actual data. You can explode bills of activity for items sold in a period and compare the result to costs of sales. Once you have a satisfactory model, use it to project the financial results of the new company. It also helps to determine which portion of operations to salvage and which, if any, to discontinue.

The example selected to illustrate the principles involved is the pro-

posed purchase of Aluminum Recycling Co. The major difference between this and other types of ABM analysis, we'll find, is in the use of
projected and probabilistic information.

ALUMINUM RECYCLING CO.

Aluminum recyclers convert beverage cans and other aluminum scrap into
secondary aluminum ingots. The product line is subject to commodity
competition. The basis for the competitive advantage is the low cost of the
scrap raw material as compared to primary metal. The margin expected on the
material is known as the **spread.**

The party interested in purchasing Aluminum Recycling Co. could add
the operation to its present ones with a $375,000 increase in supporting
activities. The purchaser's main concern is knowing how much return and risk
are involved in the investment.

As in any other application, ABM begins with an analysis of activities,
illustrated in Exhibit 11-9. In recycling, the direct activities are as follows:

  ◆ *Consuming raw material and generating scrap.* Raw material includes
aluminum scrap. Yield losses may occur at all processing stages, but, with
the exception of certain impurities known as dross, it reverts to operations
through remelting. Dross requires further processing to prepare it for reuse. The existing information system tracks weight charged and produced
through measurements at each stage of processing.

  ◆ *Melting, purchasing, receiving.* Weight of material appears to adequately account for most of the costs associated with the activities of melt,
purchasing, and receiving. At this stage, the material has commodity characteristics. In circumstances involving many transactions, as in purchasing
small quantities of beverage cans directly from consumers, these additional transaction costs would also be reflected.

  ◆ *Milling, casting.* Within the mill, ingots begin to assume some of
their final characteristics. Size is determined here, as well as composition.
Larger ingots result in higher output per minute over which to recapture
fixed costs, but they may also require additional variable costs in the form
of extra crew. Ingots produced must cool before further processing. Activity drivers include pounds and units.

  ◆ *Other activities.* The recycler may or may not perform finishing operations, such as annealing or rolling. Treatment of order activities, special
customer requirements, and inefficiencies are as described for other companies. For simplicity, these are left out of the exhibit.

Exhibit 11-9. Cost-Cause Grid: Aluminum Recycling Facility

Level II Drivers *("Cause")*	*Operating Activities* *("Cost")*
	Direct
◆ Orders	Order activities
◆ Direct charge	Material, yield loss
◆ Weight	Melting, purchasing, receiving
◆ Weight, units	Milling, casting

The model constructed to address the questions of return and risk is presented in Exhibit 11-10. While it does not offer a definite yes or no answer to whether to go ahead with the proposed investment, it does clarify the issues. On the basis of the historical distribution of spreads and anticipated operating costs, you'd expect net income of $900,000. The variability in that amount, however, is substantial, from a high of $2,325,000 net income to a low of $675,000 net loss. This variation represents the investors' risk.

ABM lets you test additional scenarios. Varying the pounds and unit output mixes will affect operating costs. This all helps to support the purchaser's decisions.

Bottlenecks

When offering multiple product lines or variations, determining your true niche is important. It may be that a seeming winner is really a loser.

Bottlenecks are operations that constrain others because of insufficient capacity. Generally, tracking and controlling queues at these operations is essential. When bottlenecks are attributable to certain customers or products, they become chargeable.

To illustrate how present systems may hide these costs, here is a case that concerns a steel manufacturer.

Exhibit 11-10. Acquisition of Aluminum Recycling Facility

Output mix assumed:
Pounds: 25,000,000
Units: 5,000

MARGIN ON RAW MATERIAL ("SPREAD")

Value Amount	Probability	Expected Value
$3,500,000	15%	$ 525,000
3,000,000	10	300,000
2,500,000	20	500,000
2,000,000	20	400,000
1,500,000	10	150,000
1,000,000	15	150,000
500,000	10%	$ 50,000
Total expected value		$2,075,000

OPERATING COSTS

Driver	Quantity	Cost Per	Extended Cost
Pounds	25,000,000	$0.02	$ 500,000
Units	5,000	60.00	300,000
Others			375,000
Total			$1,175,000
Net income			$ 900,000

While the expected annual return on the investment is $900,000, the range of possibilities is substantial. Based on historical variation, net income could be as high as $2,325,000, but as low as a loss of $675,000. Similar models would be constructed for varying output mix assumptions.

BAR SPLITTER LTD.

Bar Splitter Ltd. uses steel bars to hot roll a variety of items. Normal operations split the bars lengthwise into several pieces, each routed through its own set of rollers to take on its unique shape. Intense furnace heat is needed for splitting and rolling operations. Each line must run simultaneously at the same speed. The lines may move only as quickly as the slowest item being run, so balancing is very important.

Bar Splitter Ltd. has a highly sophisticated standard cost and variance reporting system for product costing and operational control. It treats the intense heat required to split the bars as a joint cost that should be disregarded in determining product profitability. Product costs are determined by dividing remaining operating costs by standard output for each line. For example, each line may be budgeted at $250 per hour; a product with a five-ton-per-hour standard might cost $50 per ton, and one with a ten-ton-per-hour standard would cost $25 per ton.

When high-volume items run with slow sections, an unfavorable productivity variance for the high-volume items results. While high-volume products absorb the productivity problems, slow sections show a higher profit per ton.

Intuitively, operations personnel doubt accounting's cost reports. The productivity variance comes not from less effort but from the mix of products run. Management suspects the accuracy of its reporting system, and decides to try ABM.

Results: ABM reveals the company's major costing problem: Because the lines move only as quickly as the slowest product, that product creates a bottleneck. Costs in loss of productivity for fast products may be extremely high. Using traditional joint costing, Bar Splitter's standard cost system did not reflect the true cost of the bottleneck product.

If the additional joint costs caused by the slow products are not considered in decision making, the result could be the perpetuation of unprofitable lines. From an ABM standpoint, costs should be tied to what causes them through activities and activity drivers. If an activity causes a cost to be incurred, then that cost should be charged to that activity. If a product creates a bottleneck, then that product must reflect the cost of constraining the others.

Extending this idea to joint products, if a particular product increases total joint costs, that increment should be charged to the constraining product. The slow products cause the higher costs and therefore should bear the burden. Once this is understood, the result is a radical new look at product profitability. The high-volume products are more profitable than they appear, and the slow, low-volume sections are less. This was the reality of Bar Splitter's operation, a reality that traditional accounting did not contemplate.

ABM implementation disclosed several other ways in which slow sections were subsidized:

+ The cost of yield loss allocated at an equal standard rate to all products, although far below standard for high-volume operations and above standard for low-volume ones
+ Assignment of full costs to leftover short sections arising most commonly from slow sections, although the leftovers must usually be sold at a scrap value below cost
+ Order costs associated with generating, scheduling, processing, and tracking low-volume sections, which tend to be customized
+ Costs of carrying the slower-turning slow section inventories

The cost-cause grid for Bar Splitter's direct activities is shown in Exhibit 11-11. Results of reassigning these costs are presented in Exhibit 11-12. As is evident, the profitability implications are substantial. The low-volume sections generate losses, which have been subsidized by other products. In reality, as suspected by operations personnel, the company's true niche lies elsewhere.

The problem described here does not have an easy solution. As it stands, customers of low-volume products are being subsidized at the expense of customers of high-volume products. But if production were switched entirely to high-volume products, would market demand be large enough to support the output, or would the company need to operate below its capacity? This is where the cooperation of sales and marketing is needed.

Viewed in a new way, the company could attempt to better balance its lines by running all the slow sections together. If the runs produce profit and the mill is below capacity, that solution may be a desirable one. But certainly, the present policy of mixing slow and fast sections slows the pace of the entire mill, making it seem as if only slow products are being produced. The situation is similar to one in which high-value material is substituted for low-value material in that the cost of the fast products increases because of operating inefficiency.

Using traditional systems, the management team would be unlikely to view the problem in this light. Customers of slow sections may demand expedited production calling for a mix of high- and low-volume products. For this costly inefficiency generated for the company, they probably would have been charged a nominal expediting fee rather than the share

Exhibit 11-11. Cost-Cause Grid: Bar Splitter Ltd.

Level II Drivers ("Cause")	Operating Activities ("Cost")
	Additional Direct
◆ Direct charge	Productivity inhibition
◆ Direct charge	Yield loss
◆ Direct charge	Leftover sections
◆ Slow section orders	Custom order activities
◆ Carrying rate	Storage

Exhibit 11-12. Product Profitability: Bar Splitter Ltd.

Order comparison, based on 10,000-pound (5-ton) order:

	Per Ton Basis	
Description	High-Volume	Low-Volume
Profit per ton, traditional	$160	$ 200
Changes from traditional to ABM analysis:		
Inhibited productivity	0	(40)
Actual product yield	15	(60)
Chargeable off-fall loss	5	(40)
Order cost	5	(30)
Carrying cost	15	(40)
Adjusted profit (loss) per ton	$200	$ (10)

Based on the operations of Bar Splitter Ltd., this exhibit provides a listing of the types of inefficiency that low-volume products may create and not be charged for using traditional accounting systems.

of the actual reduction in profits they should have borne. This is a situation where throughput of an entire operation has been slowed to meet the needs of a few customers.

Complexity

The effects of product-mix complexity frequently escape traditional cost systems. The following case concerns a manufacturer of decorative metal objects, which include collectibles and trophies.

DECORATIVE METALS CORP.

The issues affecting decorative metals companies were introduced in Chapter 6 in the awards manufacturer example. These companies produce standard catalog and custom items. Marketing channels are highly diverse, many of them involving small, custom quantities.

The immediate concern of Decorative Metals Corp. is costing of catalog as opposed to custom items. Each line makes up approximately half the total business, but custom work is growing rapidly. Operations expresses an intuitive awareness that the cost system is subsidizing the complexity of custom items because the cost differentials are not being factored in. Management realizes it needs ABM.

The decorative metals industry faces many complexity-cost issues. In a small-order environment, management must understand lot-based costs in order to optimize lot sizes for stock items. With regard to custom items, management is primarily concerned with the varying levels of rejects and rework, particularly if their costs have been averaged over all output through an overhead pool. Management may believe that job costing is not feasible, as it would produce a nonreviewable morass of paper.

As long as the company is profitable, the temptation may be to prepare "standards" by which to cost products and ignore actual costs, which may vary considerably. However, when the standards are labor-based and spread inefficiencies over all products, the results can be disastrous. Major items overlooked in such a system include lot-based costs like setup, nonlabor-paced operations, and inefficiencies attributable to specific orders, such as rework, rejects, expediting, and overtime.

Trying to relate a plating operation to direct labor time, for example, is a nearly hopeless task. The actual labor involved occurs in setting up the operation and handling the lot of material. This accounts for only a small part of the time the items are actually immersed in solution, during which labor may be engaged in various other projects. To apply cost on the basis of labor simply does not fit the operation; it risks a significant over- or underapplication of total departmental costs.

A traditional alternative to fitting a square cost peg into a round labor hole is simply to treat immersion operations as overhead and spread their costs across labor hours of other operations. The relative costs of plating operations, however, may be highly significant. To relegate these costs to overhead is to fail to apply a large chunk of operating costs to products.

ABM provides a practical alternative. Direct activities in the operation are as follows:

◆ *Raw material, yield loss.* Consistent with an attempt to streamline cost reporting, raw material consumption may be determined by a **back-flush method,** under which consumption is estimated by subtracting production and an assumed yield loss factor. As long as the loss factor does not include costs actually chargeable to specific customers or orders, this should not create any problems. Higher rework and scrap costs attributable to custom products must be assigned to them.

◆ *Die casting.* Once set up, modern die-casting machinery may run unattended. Rejects may occur in initial runs that form part of the initial setup cost. Therefore, lot-based costs are significant and machine run time must be distinguished from labor. Molds, mold cavities, weight, and setups are preferred for applying costs. For infrequently run custom items, the operator's lack of familiarity with the machinery may cause higher costs.

◆ *Deburring, polishing.* The complexity of the object being finished means more time spent and more inefficiencies incurred. A custom finish, for example, requires more exacting specifications than a standard one. Certain shapes, too, may be more difficult to work on.

◆ *Immersion (plating, degreasing, etc.).* The costs for immersion operations are influenced by lots, surface area, and characteristics of the required solution—including time in, temperature, and composition. Because ABM assigns costs to underlying operations, the characteristics mentioned become activity drivers. Again, certain custom activities may be infrequently performed and require rework.

◆ *Silkscreening.* Silkscreening imprints designs on metal surfaces. The time allotted to setup tends to be highly significant as the number of colors determines the number of passes. These are the important characteristics that ABM must capture as activity drivers.

◆ *Assembly, packaging.* The final operations of assembly and packaging are driven by lots, pieces, and components. Custom items require some initial getting used to.

◆ *Order and special service activities.* These constitute a high portion of total costs, due to the large volume of orders and small-order quantities involved.

The ABM cost-cause grid for Decorative Metals Corp. shown in Exhibit 11-13 addresses management's concerns. Because processing costs differ in nearly every operation according to whether the item is custom or standard catalog, the direct activities involved in each are recognized separately.

Management now has the needed information to assess its costs, profitability, and pricing.

Make-or-Buy

ABM models for make-or-buy decisions were provided in Chapter 7. One area tending toward vertical integration is the paper industry. This is the subject of the next case.

Papermilling

Papermilling is the process of producing paper rollstock or rolls from pulp. Papermaking is extremely capital-intensive, since it commonly calls for three or four production shifts to adequately utilize the investment. Papermill customers are converters who may corrugate or produce sheets, e.g., of paper. Many converters ultimately sell to box makers.

PAPER, INC.

Paper, Inc., a papermill that also distributes boxes, is considering adding a box-making operation so that it will no longer need to buy for distribution. The proposed operation would be limited to supplying internal needs so that it would not interfere with the markets of its milling customers. For ABM purposes, Paper, Inc.'s direct activities include papermilling and box distribution, as illustrated in the cost-cause grid in Exhibit 11-14. Its papermilling activities are as follows:

◆ *Raw material, preparation, yield loss.* The pulp raw material may be produced internally or externally. Weight and direct charge are bases for applying these costs.

◆ *Papermaking.* Paper machinery, including a headbox for raw material, a fourdrinier onto which the material is spread, and drums for drying,

Exhibit 11-13. Cost-Cause Grid: Decorative Metals Corp.

Level II Drivers ("Cause")	*Operating Activities* ("Cost")
	Direct: Catalog
◆ Direct charge	Material, yield loss
◆ Direct charge	Die casting
◆ Lots, surface area, solution temperature, time and composition	Immersion
◆ Passes, setups	Silk screening
◆ Lots, components, pieces	Assembly, packaging
	Direct: Custom
◆ Custom orders	Order activities
◆ Direct charge	Custom rework
◆ Direct charge	Material, yield loss
◆ Direct charge	Die casting
◆ Lots, surface area, solution temperature, time and composition	Immersion
◆ Passes, setups	Silk screening
◆ Lots, components, pieces	Assembly, packaging

produces paper having various characteristics. Weight, footage, width, and grade influence assignment of costs.

◆ *Rewinding.* The rewinding process smooths the paper and forms it into large rolls. Rolls and footage are bases for applying costs.

◆ *Slitting.* In a manner similar to that described for steel, the large rolls of paper are slit to customer order. Footage and setups are activity drivers.

◆ *Shipping.* Orders and rolls are bases for applying shipping costs.

On the distribution side, the direct activities include:

◆ *Receiving.* Receiving of finished boxes for distribution is driven by the number of loads.

Exhibit 11-14. Cost-Cause Grid: Paper Inc.

Level II Drivers ("Cause")	Operating Activities ("Cost")
	Direct: Paper Mill
• Direct charge, weight	Material, preparation, yield loss
• Weight, footage, width, grade	Paper making
• Rolls, footage	Rewinding
• Footage, setups	Slitting
• Carrying rate	Storage
• Orders	Order activities
	Direct: Distribution
• Loads	Receiving
• Carrying rate	Storage
• Orders	Order activities
• Units, distance	Order picking
• Units, MSF, weight	Packaging, shipping

♦ *Storage.* Storage should be applied at a carrying rate.
♦ *Order activities.* Number of orders are the basis for assigning order costs.
♦ *Order picking.* This activity varies with order lines and distance.
♦ *Packaging and shipping.* Units, thousands of square feet (MSF), and pounds share a role in driving the costs.

In order to fully take advantage of manufacturing for its distribution operation, Paper, Inc., needs to acquire converting as well as finishing equipment. Applying the steps given in Chapter 7, it determines the following:

Initial investment in equipment and setup:	$5,000,000
Increase in annual fixed overhead costs:	1,500,000
Increase in annual variable costs:	2,000,000

According to published industry statistics, the spread between costs of milled paper and average finished boxes amounts to approximately $5,000,000, leaving $1,500,000 annual net income, or a 30 percent return, during the life of the investment. The payback period is just under three years.

The one variable left out of the analysis is learning costs. Management believes it cannot provide a reasonable estimate, but is prepared to say that if the return falls below 25 percent, the risk is not worth taking. Given these assumptions, the high end of the learning-cost range may be calculated in a manner similar to breakeven (see Exhibit 11-15). The results indicate that the maximum learning cost needed to achieve a 25 percent return is $1,000,000. This represents less than a third of the total additional annual costs of the operation. It is reasonable to expect that the inefficiencies generated in initial operations could exceed this amount.

Results: Management decides not to pursue the decision. When utilization is inadequate to justify the costs of making rather than buying, there may be other options. Certain hospitals have added a third alternative to make-or-buy: Share. When expected utilization does not justify any single facility owning certain specialized equipment, some hospitals pool needs to support acquisitions.

Equipment Leasing

A question related to make-or-buy is leasing. For the lessor, equipment leasing has been touted as the answer to tax reform. In what appears to be a win-win situation, lessors obtain the tax benefits of owning equipment together with a steady cash flow, whereas lessees fulfill their needs with no money down. But unless the lease is structured for protection, the lessor can be badly burned.

Computer leasing, the single largest category of equipment leased in the United States, is subject to special circumstances. You will recall from the discussion of lease-or-buy decisions that it is more beneficial to lease

---

Exhibit 11-15. Make-or-Buy Decision: Paper, Inc.

Annual net income	$1,500,000
Required return during life	÷ 25%
Maximum initial investment	$6,000,000
Less equipment and setup portion	(5,000,000)
Maximum learning costs	$1,000,000

One way to estimate the impact of learning costs is to set an upper limit and assess its reasonableness. Here, the amount indicated is reasonable, but it is outside of management's tolerance.

where technology is rapidly advancing. The point at which the present value of lease payments equals the purchase price of the equipment is likely to occur *after* the point of technological change. It is the lessors of computer equipment, not lessees, who bear this risk.

The problems may have led lessors to delineate the sources of their profits. Installation of computer systems tend to incur costs that are more predictable and are therefore more likely to attain target profits. Similarly, service contracts may be somewhat more predictable and able to protect the lessor. A mere lease of equipment does not absorb much risk.

Alternatives include attaching a number to this risk and building it into the lease. The lessor can share the risk with the lessee by extending the noncancelable term of the lease or having the lessee guarantee the equipment's residual value. Lessors may also consider structuring leases as sales.

12

Sustaining High Productivity and Service with ABM

Chapters 1 through 11 have given you a tour through the ABM world. You may find some parts may be clearer than others, and you may need to revisit others later.

ABM is meant to support continuous improvement in operations. Once you have exposed the most glaring inefficiencies, you should continue on to new areas. And your model, subject to continuous validation, should adapt accordingly.

It is unlikely that your model will stabilize for at least a few months, but once it has, it will be ready for any application, including support of strategic decisions. By then, your niche markets will have become clear, costs will be manageable, and a new information consciousness will have emerged.

The next move is yours. Remember, ABM is most effective when it involves all functional areas. The results can be shocking. Without sufficient support and participation, the new information will not be acted upon, which is why ABM implementation really calls for a cross-functional task force.

If you want immediate results but are at a loss as to what to do next, turn to Compendium I for a five-step shortcut to immediate cost management. Other ideas are likely to occur to you in the process.

ABM represents the dawning of a new age in management information. Made possible by technology, it will finally reach its full potential.

Appendix
Where Accounting
Has Gone Wrong

Fifty years ago, accounting students read about job costing, process costing, budgeting, and standard costing with variance analysis. An examination of today's texts shows that very little has changed. The ideas illustrated are identical with those from early in this century. But while accounting has not changed, the industries that it models have changed dramatically. Today, major industries rely on automation as much as they once did on manual labor. Cost systems are as obsolete as the labor-intensive operations that they once represented.

Your cost system determines the quality of information provided for decision making. This appendix is devoted to analyzing the inadequacies of traditional approaches.

You have probably heard the phrase "one size fits all." It usually refers to very cheap clothing. The most sought-after clothing, in contrast, is tailored or customized. In some ways, traditional accounting is a one-size-fits-all approach. Just as human beings are too diverse to fit one shirt size, so companies do not fit one financial model.

The only redeeming thing about traditional systems is their extreme simplicity. However, such oversimplifications are unnecessary today. Traditional methods originated in the days of completely manual bookkeeping, when companies required large staffs to perform the equivalent level of work of a single data processor at a computer terminal. These systems are as obsolete as the pen-and-ink ledgers in which they were recorded. Yet training for accountants has not yet adapted to new management needs or system capabilities.

Financial Reporting

Financial reporting illustrates the one-size-fits-all idea. It is so generic that distinguishing one company or industry from another is difficult. It's rooted in early information systems that focused not on operations but on accounting needs. Banks, investors, and the IRS naturally had to be the first ones satisfied, but many systems stopped there. External reporting was also used internally. It failed to identify controllable costs or relationships between costs and the activities that caused them.

Do you get the information needed to run a business from financial reports? Consider the typical financial statement in Exhibit A-1. Most notable is the extremely high level of aggregation. The cost-of-sales numbers result from production costs give or take the change in inventories for the period. They are not intended to represent the costs that attached to goods sold during the period, but rather are an amalgamation of whatever is not capitalized into ending inventory. This camouflages controllable costs.

For example, the amount of metal in a product comes from the product's specifications, but metal lost due to operator error doesn't. Controllable costs, such as special customer services and waste, are aggregated with those expected to be in the product. Other examples of controllable costs include:

- ◆ *Raw material.* Scrap, shrinkage, quality substitution, volume discounts, inventory policies
- ◆ *Direct labor.* Downtime, overtime, setup, handling, rework, underutilized skills, production problems, lack of training
- ◆ *Overhead.* An aggregation of items neglected in traditional costing, e.g., costs of carrying assets, idle capacity, and a multitude of issues relating to the specific character of these costs

What accountants call **overhead** on a financial statement is an extremely diverse and significant category of costs, as analyzed in Exhibit A-2. Financial statement treatment is almost as ridiculous as the story in which the treasurer announces the three expenses for the year: telephone calls, 60 cents; pencils, 20 cents; and miscellaneous, $3,000,000.

Included in manufacturing overhead are costs of idle capacity, rework, automation, administration, occupancy, indirect payroll and material costs, tooling, and supplies, among others. Financial statements treat overhead in a summary fashion, without regard for these components. Analyzing them as a ratio to labor, as many systems do, offers little or no insight into their causes and no means of controlling them.

Certainly, you will not find information for managing costs in typical external user reports. Managers who look for more details are generally directed to cost systems, including budgeting and product cost information.

Exhibit A-1. Sample Generic Financial Statement

Sales		$10,000,000
Cost of sales:		
Material	$3,005,000	
Direct labor	979,000	
Overhead	$4,044,000	
Total		8,028,000
Gross profit		1,972,000
Selling, general, and administrative		1,615,000
Net earnings		$ 357,000

This sample financial statement aptly illustrates the generic reporting generated by accounting. Managers are left hungry for more information. In turning to traditional cost systems, they do not find it.

Exhibit A-2. Manufacturing Overhead Costs

- Downtime, rework, and scrap
- Machinery and equipment costs such as depreciation, maintenance, supplies, energy, and related indirect labor
- Plant administration, including management, supervision, scheduling, production control, and inspection
- Occupancy costs such asbuilding depreciation, maintenance, rent, real estate taxes, security, and utilities
- Payroll-related costs, including payroll taxes, benefits, holiday and overtime pay, pensions, and union costs
- Material-related costs, including insurance, personal property taxes, and material-handling personnel and equipment
- Supplies, tools, dies, spare parts, and indirect materials

Costs classified as overhead are highly diverse. The traditional approach to these costs applies them over a single base. Although inappropriate, this approach is all that traditional systems offer

Budgeting

The constant surprises found in month-end financial statements are not lessened by budgeting. Traditional budgeting is most aptly described as a half-hearted attempt to provide management with information for planning and control that is missing from financial reports. The flexible budget compares production costs with a budget that varies depending on the level of volume measured in sales, direct labor hours, or units. But like traditional methods of calculating costs for products, flexible budgeting is a one-base approach.

Trying to gain operational and planning insight from traditional methods is like using a shotgun to remove a hangnail: This was not the original purpose of an imprecise tool. Traditional systems were designed to provide a largely oversimplified level of pseudo-control, not as a means for understanding the causes of costs. The most sophisticated traditional systems distinguish between **variable costs**, meaning those that change in linear relation to volume, and **fixed costs,** meaning for all other items of expense. Line items of variable manufacturing costs are assigned budget allowances that vary in relation to equivalent units or, more commonly, sales volume in dollars. Exhibit A-3 shows the familiar conventional approach, which ties budgets for variable expenses to a percentage of sales and relegates fixed amounts to the nonvariable categories.

For any company that produces more than a single, homogeneous product, these systems fail to reflect changes in product mix. An approach so simplified cannot possibly account for the complexity of cost behavior. Moreover, while it is useful to break costs down into components of those that vary with sales and those that remain fixed as volume changes, for many expenses the distinction blurs. Those called variable, such as direct labor and material, never increase and decrease in exact proportion to sales. Most costs relate to specific activities, not total volume.

Detailed Costing

Cost systems are intended to provide product cost and operational information to management, which requires bases or common denominators for relating costs to products. Traditional cost systems rely on a single base for this function. For process costing, used in line and continuous operations, the base is units produced; for job costing, used in project, job, and batch operations, it is material for actual charges and direct labor for all other costs.

Exhibit A-3. Sample Traditional Budget

Sales	100%	$10,000,000
Cost of sales:		
Material	30%	3,000,000
Direct labor	10%	1,000,000
Overhead—variable	25%	2,500,000
Overhead—fixed	fixed	1,500,000
Total		8,000,000
Gross profit		2,000,000
Selling, general and administrative	fixed	1,500,000
Net earnings		$ 500,000

Traditional budgeting is another illustration of an oversimplified approach. Flexible budgets vary either with volume in sales or units. Actual cost drivers are much more diverse.

What this means is that diverse overhead costs are all applied in one way: to products using a single base. If conversion costs total $10 million, job costing spreads them over 100,000 budgeted chargeable hours for a rate of $100 per hour. For an order requiring ten labor hours, $1,000 would be applied in overhead. Process costing similarly would apply the conversion costs on the basis of one million budgeted units, for a rate of $10 per unit.

Let's look at process- and job-costing systems more closely, followed by absorption, standard costing, reporting problems, and cost analyses. Then, we'll discuss common system deficiencies and the techniques used in practice.

Process Costing

Process costing is used in repetitive or flow production environments. It uses units as the basis for allocating costs, as the assumed similarity of end items would not justify direct charging of time or material. A major decision is the definition of *units:* pieces? weight? length? Because a single unit base must represent all output, the selection of the one size meant to fit all is never clear-cut. For process costing to work, a company must produce a single product. Otherwise, stating costs per unit or per ton or per something else is highly misleading.

The fallacy of this technique is again in the assumption that one size (hour, unit) fits all—that each pound or unit or hour incurs equal cost. Only the costs of single-product firms could possibly behave in such a manner.

Process costing spreads certain costs of highest concern, like down-time, setup, overtime, and rework, across the entire product mix. This means that inefficiency and waste, which in reality are attributable to a specific customer, lot size, or order complexity, appear in the costs of all products. In competitive times, this may cause companies to turn down profitable business.

Job Costing

The difference between job costing and process costing is that job costing charges direct labor time and material costs by order. While this type of system requires substantial extra effort to obtain the additional detail, the focus is on material and labor, not automation and other overhead. The ever-increasing pool of overhead is dealt with in a manner similar to that of process costing. Inefficiency, automation, and other diverse costs are aggregated and averaged across all production, which potentially could so inflate bids on high-volume production as to render the company un-competitive.

Implicit in job costing is the idea that overhead costs are somehow generated by labor. If Joe from welding charges three hours to job A and John from finishing charges seventeen, the overhead applied to the job is twenty hours times the overhead rate of $100, or $2,000. One rate and one method fit all operations. For payroll fringe items, such as payroll taxes, group medical insurance, and pensions, basing overhead on labor hours may be logical. For other overhead costs, the relationship to labor is tenuous at best.

Parts requiring high machining would not bear their share of over-head costs, whereas those requiring more assembly would be correspondingly overcharged. Similarly, custom items would incur more overhead in the form of supervision, rework, and so on. Under a single rate system, those items would be undercharged, whereas high-volume stock items would be overcharged.

Also, job costing excludes general and administrative items from costing altogether. This is true even when certain costs may vary based on orders.

Cost Application

At this point, you may be asking, "How have auditors, investors, banks and the IRS tolerated these distortions all these years?" The answer is simple: Accounting principles do not mandate proper cost allocation among products. Instead, they identify certain costs that must be applied to inventory, leaving the details to the user. Manufacturing costs are misapplied when the amount applied to all products differs significantly from the amount incurred or that should be incurred based on decisions being made.

Auditors generally test application of costs. This means calculating how much of a particular cost was applied to production and comparing it to actual costs. The difference is either over- or underabsorbed. If the amount is significant, auditors record an adjustment to decrease or increase inventory, an adjustment not usually reflected in the detailed cost records for the year.

Here's an example: Chargeable labor hours carry a burden rate of $80 per hour. If 100,000 hours of production occur during the year, a total of $8,000,000 ($80 times 100,000 hours) is absorbed by production. If actual overhead expenses are $6,972,000, overhead is overapplied by $1,028,000, meaning product costs applied are higher than their actual costs. Conversely, if actual overhead is higher, budgeted overhead is underapplied.

More sophisticated systems monitor cost application monthly. Large monthly variances are a sign that the base (hours, units) is probably inappropriate for representing the causal relationship to cost.

Another aspect of application is the treatment of abnormal costs and idle capacity. If a company in its start-up year builds a facility with 100,000 units annual capacity and incurs $250,000 in direct labor costs as a result of learning how to use the equipment, how much of these costs should you apply to units produced, assuming only one good unit is completed? If you apply the entire amount and price on that basis, you'll never sell a unit. Recall the idea of a normal volume or level of activity from Chapter 3.

Standard Costing

The most sophisticated traditional reporting system of standard costing and variance analysis offers little chance for improved information. The idea is a defined budgeted quantity expressed in labor hours or units, and a defined budgeted cost rate related to production of a certain item. For example, our standard is that product A takes 20 labor hours at a rate of $10 per hour. If it takes 25 hours and the rate averages $12 because of some overtime, our actual cost to produce A becomes $300 (25 hours times $12) compared to the standard cost of $200 (20 hours times $10). The idea of variance analysis is to break out how much of the unfavorable difference of $100 is attributable to a higher average pay rate and how much to lower productivity. We paid an average of $2 more per hour than we budgeted; therefore, $2 times our actual hours of 25 explains $50 of the $100. We worked an extra 5 hours at a budgeted rate of $10, which explains the other $50. Overhead variances are analyzed the same way, using the basis defined in product costing, either labor hours or units.

Standards reporting is the classic carrot-and-stick approach. Variances not explained by "price" must occur in "productivity." To get better performance, you raise the productivity standard. Labor conforms by doctoring records: A generous time allowance given for one product is saved for the overage on another product. You legislate behavior, but you lose the element of understanding that is needed for true control.

The dream of **management by exception** envisioned a reporting system in which managers would receive accounts of variances out of tolerance, for immediate action. The dream could not be realized with a system so oversimplified that to miss the mark was the norm, not the exception, particularly for overhead budgeted on labor or units.

Other Reporting System Deficiencies

Financial Indicators

While nothing is wrong with financial ratios and indicators per se, the data used in them derive from financial information that conforms with generally accepted accounting principles (**GAAP**). Where GAAP assumptions are overly conservative, the resulting statistical interpretations suffer from the deficiency.

For example, return on assets (ROA) suffers from short-sightedness, but it is widely used in evaluating managers. **ROA** is the ratio of pretax net income to total assets, which could just as well be used to evaluate investment portfolios. What limits its usefulness it how GAAP defines net income and assets. As discussed in Chapter 7, expenditures on research, employee development, preventive maintenance, or any number of other forward-looking improvements are treated not as assets but as expenses deducted from net income, in the same manner as office supplies or rent. Yet, the former are investments in the future, and the latter a cost of the present. Likewise, ROA favors fully depreciated machinery, even though applying the resources elsewhere would be more productive.

Under these systems, managers develop an attitude toward long-term projects as being just wishful thinking. An evaluation based on ROA constrains them to quick fixes. In contrast, a different incentive could offer room to innovate, experiment, and invest in the long term.

Managers can also manipulate ROA or inventory measures. Inventory-costing games give the appearance of an improved bottom line. For example, production can create income. Because fixed costs are based on budgeted rates, excessive production causes the fixed costs added to inventory to exceed costs incurred during the month, and building up inventory heightens financial position. Conversely, lack of production can also create income. If the bottom has fallen out on volume, the accountants may implement a new, higher rate for applying fixed costs over a lower volume. Revaluing opening inventory at the higher rates results in significant and immediate increases in income.

Standard Cost-Variance Analysis

Variance analysis in standard costing is also deficient in several areas, as follows:

◆ Measures are labor–time-based, inhibiting understanding of actual production operations, methods, and peculiarities. Activities and drivers relating to overhead are not analyzed.

◆ Standards are developed usually as a one-shot investment that may be so expensive that updating is discouraged. Under these circumstances, standards do not adapt to changes in the business.

◆ Inefficiency and scrap are built into the standards as allowances. This does nothing to encourage improved efficiency.

◆ Variances may arise out of inaccuracies of the bases for applying cost, changes in product mix, or any of numerous other factors. The model is not adjusted for the additional activity drivers.

◆ Inefficiency and profitability impacts may be hidden by the system. Recall the many examples in Chapter 5, and the Bar Splitter Ltd. example from Chapter 11, in which unfavorable productivity variances charged to a high-volume product actually resulted from the constraining effect of a low-volume one. Likewise, frequent rework of one product may be buried in the unfavorable productivity variance of another.

◆ Generally, the data are disseminated too late to be acted upon.

Productivity Indicators

While there is nothing inherently wrong with measuring productivity, it should not be the only indicator. Just as the incentives analyzed in Chapter 9 motivated employees toward counterproductive actions, so a manager evaluated on keeping people busy is led to ignore other things. Managers held accountable for earned hours and machine utilization will encourage the building of excess inventories and, just as detrimentally, discourage long-term process improvements that may hinder productivity initially. When top executives realize this is happening, the system can change, which means better company performance in the long run.

Labor Distribution

Traditional systems measure the ratio of indirect to direct labor as if any indirect function is undesirable. The fact is, indirect labor is as essential in automated operations as direct labor is in manual ones.

Fixed and Variable Cost Analysis

While the ideas have a place in ABM, traditional analysis of fixed and variable costs is inadequate.

Traditional Approach

Fixed costs may be defined as those that do not vary in relationship to another variable, traditionally sales volume, over the period appropriate for the decision. They may or may not be controllable by management. Naturally, for some decisions, such as scheduling for next week, direct labor would be considered fixed, except for overtime. For production decisions for the next five years, on the other hand, practically all costs are variable.

Accountants commonly narrow the distinction between fixed and variable to a reasonably short-term horizon, usually one year. Costs that vary with the level of sales volume are called variable; those that don't are considered fixed. Accountants tend to classify direct material, supplies, certain maintenance, certain energy, and labor as variable, and occupancy costs, depreciation, and plant supervision as fixed.

In a similar line of thought, traditional ideas say that costs incurred in simultaneously producing multiple products should be disregarded in further decisions based on cost or profitability. Like costs, allocation does not have meaning, because the costs will continue regardless.

An alternative to this classification is to derive from historical experience how costs vary with volume. This can be by visual estimate, high-low method, or statistically, using regression analysis. Some argue that this is the only way to classify costs accurately. For example, the "direct labor" in a small retail store is two clerks, which traditional accounting would classify as variable. In reality, however, the necessity of having at least one clerk always minding the store, together with the need for lunch, bathroom, and coffee breaks, ensures that these costs are fixed.

To illustrate the high-low method, let's say that we're relating maintenance cost to machine run time in hours. The high-low method would proceed to select the highest and lowest machine hours in our set of data. If hours are 14,000 high and 10,000 low, relating to maintenance costs of $30,000 and $24,000, the variable element is the $6,000 change in cost caused by the 4,000 change in hours, or $1.50 per hour. At 14,000 hours, $21,000 variable cost is incurred; at 10,000 hours, the variable cost is $15,000. The remaining $9,000 from both cases is fixed.

Problems with the Traditional Approach

Traditional ideas of fixed and joint product costs suffer from oversimplicity, not only from an empirical standpoint but in their underlying assumptions.

One danger of using history is you're likely to be left with bad data. If, for example, salaries of a crew of four maintenance people did not change for an entire year, the model would reflect them entirely as fixed costs. To truly be accurate, some form of time reporting must be in place by which to capture downtime, time spent on building maintenance, time spent on preventive maintenance as opposed to breakdowns, etc.

Another danger of using history is hidden activity drivers. The traditional approach constrains you to volume measures, leaving out the various activities and activity drivers defined in ABM. From an ABM standpoint, the costs may not be fixed but in fact driven by other factors. Eight hours of maintenance time may be required each Saturday for changeover, for example.

The assumption that everything either varies with sales or doesn't creates a false dilemma. Too many companies, once defining costs as fixed, fall into the dangerous practice of ignoring these costs as uncontrollable. These companies miss the point.

Other factors, i.e., activity drivers, are involved, which ABM uncovers.

Moreover, incremental costs may actually be chargeable, as in the case of joint product costs. Recall the example of Bar Splitter Ltd. in Chapter 11. To exclude joint cost from the analysis is a serious mistake.

Common Deficiencies in Costing

As previously stated, the cost problem is one of oversimplification, which the power of today's computer systems can easily remedy. Examples of some problems to watch for in your system follow, and are summarized in Exhibit A-4.

♦ *Oversimplified operation or product mix that limits costing to one base.* Traditional systems, being single-based, tempt companies to do this. In the extreme, tons could be used to cost all processes regardless of how costs are incurred.

♦ *Use of a plantwide rate.* This is almost as bad as the single-product-firm assumption. For one rate to work like a multiple-rate system, every product has to spend an equal mix of its total time in each department; for example, 25 percent in machining. Distortions occur to the extent the mix of time varies.

♦ *Failure to distinguish alternate processes.* This is a problem similar to that caused by using a single rate. Here, a manual operation and its new automated alternative use the same overhead rate, because they are both classified in the same department. The mistake caused by burdening a manual operation with heavy automation costs is obvious.

♦ *Arbitrary allocation of service overhead.* Maintenance, supervision, and other general overhead expenses are often allocated to departments on the basis of their labor hours, or even equally among all departments. This technique fails to reflect the true incurrence of cost, as machinery tends to need more maintenance and less supervision than people do.

♦ *Burdening of small, complex, custom, or low-volume product orders.* Small orders often generate the same administrative effort in scheduling, order processing, billing, and so on as large orders. Complex, custom, and low-volume orders usually require more engineering, low-volume raw material, supervision, rework, and scrap costs. Traditional systems either classify these costs as administrative and ignore them for costing, or they add them to the overhead pool to be spread among all products on the basis of labor or units.

♦ *Reflection of varying material and scrap costs.* Too often, material costs and scrap rates are averaged according to some kind of standard. Further investigation may show that the higher costs averaged in with the low have definite causes. If attributable to one type of product, why average them over all products?

Exhibit A-4. Common Deficiencies in Costing

---

1. Single-base systems.
2. Plantwide costing rates.
3. Failure to distinguish between alternative processes, such as new and old technology in the same department.
4. Arbitrary allocation of service overhead, such as supervision, maintenance, and occupancy. An example of arbitrary allocation is charging equal amounts to each operation.
5. Undercosting small, complex, custom, or low-volume work.
6. Failure to reflect varying material and scrap costs.
7. Using direct labor hours in costing automated operations that have more or less than one operator per machine.
8. Failure to reflect lot costs, like setup.
9. Using plantwide average labor rate.
10. Lack of analysis of completed orders for profit contribution and comparison to initial estimates.
11. Rates out of date or not compared to financial records.
12. Rates understated by not reflecting chargeability.

Deficiencies in costing with respect to modern operations are quite common. They point up the need for a comprehensive new costing approach.

◆ *Using direct labor hours in costing automated operations.* Problems with labor-hour bases arise when the number of operators is larger or smaller than the number of machines operated. If a machine requires four operators with overhead applied equally on their labor hours, four times the burden is applied to that machine for each hour run than to one operated by a single laborer. Similarly, if an operator runs multiple machines and logs time on each one, payroll and fringe costs are overapplied and costs of operation exceed reality.

◆ *Failure to reflect lot costs.* Some companies include setup as an overhead item rather than charge particular products or orders. This is particularly common when setup personnel are separate from direct labor and are classified as "indirect labor." This tends to make short runs appear more profitable than they actually are.

Exhibit A-5. Costing Methods Used by Mid-Size Companies

PROCESS MANUFACTURING

1. *Gross profit.* Similar to retail accounting, goods are extended at their selling price and adjusted to cost by applying an average margin.

2. *Equivalent units.* Plantwide or departmental rates are determined from costs divided by the defined *equivalent unit,* based on an average.

3. *Earned hours.* Departmental or direct labor time by product or operation is derived from standards obtained through work measurement studies.

4. *Standard costing.* Earned hours are taken a step further in providing budgeted costs to which actual operating results are compared. This provides the data for exception variance reporting.

JOB OR PROJECT COSTING

1. *Labor costing.* Direct labor and material are charged by order, and overhead is either ignored or applied at a single rate.

2. *Departmental labor costing.* This method adds recognition of varying departmental overhead costs in its rates.

3. *Work-center costing.* Sophistication increases as machine hours may be added as a costing base or standards for certain repetitive operations may be established.

4. *Overhead budgeting.* This is the job shop's version of standard costing. Because jobs may vary too much to allow for a complete standard cost system, budgeted rates are used.

This may give rise to comparisons of actual and estimated costs that take on the character of variance reporting.

A number of variations on traditional systems are used by mid-size companies. The most common costing methods also tend to be the least sophisticated. Management's dissatisfaction comes as no surprise.

- *Plantwide average labor rates.* Where mixes of skills and rates differ, averages are seldom adequate. Ideally, costing should reflect the actual rates of the employees doing the job.

- *Lack of completed order analysis.* Analysis of orders should indicate their contribution to profit and performance relative to initial estimates. To prevent recurrence, scrap and downtime should be tracked and evaluated as to cause.

◆ *Rates out of date or not compared to financial records.* This provides a test of the information being provided by the cost system. Even under a perfect cost system, seldom does a company remain so stable it does not need to update costs.

◆ *Rates understated from failing to reflect chargeability.* A common error in job-cost overhead rate calculation is dividing overhead by total direct labor, without regard to the nonchargeable portion. Typically, 20 percent or more of labor time charged to jobs consists of breaks, downtime, cleanup, maintenance, and other indirect operations, which should all be treated as part of overhead. The effect can be significant. For example, overhead of $275,000 divided by $100,000 total direct labor may seem to indicate a 275 percent overhead rate. If direct labor is 75 percent chargeable, however, adjusted overhead becomes $300,000 divided by $75,000 chargeable direct labor, for a true rate of 400 percent.

Evaluating Your System

While all of this may seem rather intimidating, realize that there is no monopoly on inadequate methods. The most oversimplified techniques are also among the most widely used. Exhibit A-5 summarizes methods used by medium-size companies that responded to a survey I reported in the December 1991 issue of *APICS: The Performance Advantage.* Most manufacturers fell within the first two most unsophisticated methods, despite increasing management concerns about the effectiveness of their cost management and information systems.

Index